D0847034

MZA ABDULLAH:
E +FOLLOW ME

A Memoir. The NFL.
sition. A Challenge. A Change.

NRC CASS COUNTY PUBLIC LIBRARY
400 E. MECHANIC
HARRISONVILLE, MO 64701

0 0022 0472204 1

Hamza Abdullah: Come Follow Me—A Memoir. The NFL. A T[...]
A Change.

Copyright © 2016 by Hamza Abdullah. All rights reserved.

Obscene language appears in this text at the disapproval of the a[...]
the authenticity of the situation. The text has been include[...]
been ~~stricken~~ through.

Visit Abdullah Bros Books online at www.AbdullahBros.com.

Abdullah Bros Books and the Abdullah Bros logo are owned a[...]
Abdullah Bros.

Cover design by Twin Art Design. Cover design includes imagery f[...]
Empipe

Compiled and organized by Baiyinah Siddeeq.

Edited by Jamilah El-Amin.

Flaps and back cover written by Alexa Abdullah and Umm Zakiyyah.

Qur'an verses taken from *The Qur'an: A New Translation by M. A. S.*
copyright © 2004, 2005, 2010 by M. A. S. Abdel-Haleem.

The stories in this book are about real people, real events and real circums[...]
names, teams and/or position of other players have been changed to protect th[...]
the individuals involved.

The coaching statistics have been compiled by Mustafa Johnwell and are availabl[...]
on www.AbdullahBros.com. Statistics are accurate as of September 11, 2016. A[...]
2% for general oversight.

Hardcover
ISBN: 978-0-9981129-0-9

Paperback
ISBN: 978-0-9981129-1-6

e-Book
ISBN: 978-0-9981129-2-3

Printed in the United States of America

To my wife Alexa,
who followed me when no one else would.

TABLE OF CONTENTS

In the name of God, the Lord of Mercy, the Giver of Mercy

"If you don't help yourself now, you won't be able to help anyone else in the future."
—Steve Sanders, Training Camp for Life

INTRODUCTION

I spent seven years in the NFL, five years at Washington State University, two years in high school, and three years in Pop Warner learning selflessness and leadership. The skills I learned on the football field helped propel me to a leadership role off of it. I was voted team captain in college and served as a mentor during my NFL days. I learned the best way to lead was to "want for my brother what I wanted for myself." I wanted to be successful on and off the field. It didn't always work out the way I planned but through hard work and consistency, I was able to carve out a respectable balance.

By showing my selflessness, other players trusted me, believed in me, and eventually followed me. With this trust came a huge responsibility that has only been magnified since I retired. The NFL players' transition story needs to be told, and the transition system needs to be changed. Now that playing the game is not an option, many players look to me to guide them from the valley of darkness, to the Promised Land. I have taken the challenge and have spent the years since I retired reading, writing, and researching different ways to best navigate this Transition. With the help of God, I pray that we can all reach the Promised Land safely. Grab only what you can carry because it will be an arduous journey. Make sure you bring your compassion, empathy and heart. When it feels as though you can no longer go on, promise me that you will remember the people who came before you and those that will come after. The ones before persisted to make a way, and the ones behind will never know the way if we desert it now. We can do it, and we will do it. God willing.

I am your brother and my number one priority is your safety. Trust me and...

Come follow me.

PART ONE

LIFE IS ABOUT TRANSITION

"Change is an inevitable part of life...Life is easier when we accept these changes and recognize how every moment of our journey is an important part of the growth of our soul."
—Muhammad Ali, *The Soul of a Butterfly*

1

TRANSITION?

My first transition happened in 1989 when I was six years old. That's when my mother and father divorced. I was tied with my twin sister Hajirah for being the second oldest of six children. Four boys and two girls ranging in ages from newborn to eight. The six children—Abbas, Hajirah, Hamza, Husain, Shaybah, and Aliyyah—along with my parents, crammed into a small two bedroom apartment in Pomona, CA.

We spent our days commuting to Los Angeles in a Toyota Tercel hatchback and our nights wondering where my father was, what he was doing, and who he was doing it with. One night I heard my parents going at it.

"Where are you going?"
"Don't question me."
"You're leaving us here all by ourselves."
"You know I have things to do."
"What about us? What about your family?"
"I told you already, I have things to do."
"And we're supposed to be sitting here hungry, waiting on you?"
"I'm leaving..."
"Then leave...and don't come back...but you can't take my car."
"Listen woman..."
"Leave!"
"I said..."
"Leave!"
"Woman!"
"Ahhhhhh..."

My mother let out a pained screech I hadn't heard before. I walked out of the room and saw my mother crying. She told me to go back to bed. I looked at my father but he couldn't look me in the eyes. I wondered what would make a father not be able to look his six year old son in the eyes.

I didn't see much of my father after that night, and I'm not so sure that was a bad thing. I later learned that what I overheard that night was domestic violence. I wondered where we would go from here. Where would my mother go, my family and me? How do we transition to a single parent household with six young children?

Here we go.

2

CHINO

O
n June 4, 1990, my mother woke us up early and dressed us in nice clothes. We drove 15 minutes from Pomona to Chino, CA. We arrived at the California Institution for Men, or "Chino," as we knew it. It was my first time in a prison, and I prayed it would be my last. I wondered why in the world we had to put on nice clothes to visit a prison. As we walked through the security lines, we were greeted by grim-faced guards. My mother brought a cake with her, and one of the guards took a flat needle file and began stabbing the cake with it. I was petrified. What kind of place would do that to a cake? A prison would, I'd later understand. A place built to profit off creating career criminals under the guise of rehabilitation. This was no place for a cake or a child. We left the security area and headed for the yard. What was to come, I never imagined.

"*Assalamu Alaikum.*"
"*Wa alaikumu salaam.*"
"When you greet someone, look them in their eyes."
"Okay."
"Stand straight up and give them a firm handshake...like this." He took my small right hand in his, squeezing firmly, and shook once in an up and down motion.
"Okay."
"And when you're talking to a man, say, 'yes sir.'"
"Ok...Yes sir."
"There you go. What's your name?"
"Hamza."

"Hamza! You have to say it with some bass in your voice."

"Hamza!"

"There you go, Hamza."

"My name is Brother Yusuf. I'm going to be marrying your mom."

"You...You, you are?" I asked with a furrowed brow.

I wasn't ready for that. I wasn't ready for this stranger—adorned in prison blue—to tell me he was marrying my mother. I wondered what that meant for me. What it meant for my family and what it meant for my mother.

"Your mother talks about you guys all the time."

"Thank you...I guess."

"You have any questions for me?"

"Yes—what's going to happen to our family?"

"Well, when I get out of here, I'm going to come stay with you guys and help your mom out."

"Okay...uh...yes sir?"

"No, you don't have to say 'yes sir' to that.

"Okay."

"But I want you guys to call me Abu Shante."

"Abu Shante?"

"Yeah. I have other children, and my oldest child's name is Shante. So it just means: Father of Shante."

"Yes sir...okay...yes sir."

Abu Shante chuckled, "You'll get it. In the meantime, won't you go run around. I'm going to go talk with your mom."

"Yes sir."

"*Assalamu Alaikum.*"

"*Wa alaikumu salam.*"

I knew my father hadn't been around, but I didn't expect another man to enter our household. I wondered what Abu Shante's motivation was. Did he love my mom as much as I loved her? He must have. I didn't realize it at the time, but Abu Shante was the strongest man I ever knew. I couldn't think of another man who would marry a woman who already had six children. I learned a valuable lesson that day: don't judge a man by his dress or his current circumstances. Those things are superficial and can be changed as long as the person's heart is set on changing. Abu Shante wanted to change, but he started with us. He now had to raise another six children, four of them boys. He wanted us to change from mama's boys into men.

I was preparing for another transition.

3
100

Abu Shante had his work cut out for him when he was released. Not only did he have to find adequate work, he also had to raise four African-American boys in a tumultuous climate. The summer of 1991 was rough for all Southern Californians, but mostly for the African-American community. Earlier that spring, Rodney King was beaten by Los Angeles Police Department officers, resulting in heightened animosity from Blacks towards police officers.

All African-American males between the ages of eight and 28 fit the police profile of a gangster. Gangs capitalized on this overall resentment toward authority and began recruiting young black boys. The rival gangs that spread throughout Los Angeles County were the Bloods and the Crips. Bloods were identified by the primary color red, and the Crips were identified by the color blue. "Is you Blood or Cuz?" The answer to that question could lead you to a beatdown, a mugging, or a bullet.

Abu Shante taught us to say, "I'm Muslim. I don't bang."

"Hamza?"
"Yes sir?"
"Drop down and give me 100."
"One hundred?"
"Yes sir. Drop down and give me 100 push-ups."
"Wh-why 100 push-ups sir?"
"Because you need to be strong. I ain't raising no punks."
"Yes sir."
"You have to be strong out there. You can't go crying to your mom all the time."

15

"Yes sir."

"You're a soldier. You're a Muslim."

"Yes sir."

"When one of these guys roll up on you, you have to be strong. Tell them you're Muslim."

"Yes sir."

"When I was inside, I rolled with the Muslims. They protected me and they will protect you."

"Yes sir."

"We have to be strong men and strong Muslims."

"Yes sir."

"But let me tell you a secret. It's going to take more than push-ups to make you strong. You'll see when you get older."

"Yes sir."

"But in the meantime, drop and give me those 100 you owe me."

"Yes sir."

4

FOOTBALL PHOBIA

B y 1994 there were three more boys added to the family. Esa, Salih and Mustafa. We moved to a bigger home equipped with four bedrooms and two bathrooms. With a house of seven boys and three girls, Abu Shante needed a way to keep us off the streets and build toughness. He did what most reasonable fathers in the neighborhood did. He put us in sports.

"Abbas! Hamza! Husain!"
"Yes sir?" We answered in unison.
"Get your stuff together. We're going to sign you guys up for football."
"Uhh...football?" I asked.
"Yeah. Football. Boy don't act like you don't know what football is." Abu Shante said balling up his fist.
"No sir, I know what football is. I just don't really want to play it." I retorted.
I *had* wanted to play when I was younger, but in the fickleness of youth I had given up the idea. The sport seemed way to intimidating now, so maybe it wasn't for me after all.

"Boy, did I ask you? Get your stuff ready." Abu Shante shot back.
"Abu Shante, I don't really want to play either." Husain chimed in.
"What? Abbas, you too?" Abu Shante asked with hope in his tone.
"No, I want to play." Abbas said brimming with confidence.
"Well, you two squares get out of my face. Let's go, Abbas." Abu Shante said with a peeved tone.

When the opportunity to play football first came to my doorstep, I ran and hid. I didn't want any parts of hitting someone else or, more importantly, getting hit by someone else.

I focused my attention on basketball. I knew Abu Shante wanted us to play sports, so I had high hopes of starring on the neighborhood basketball team. After the first day of basketball tryouts, the coach informed us there was a 20 dollar sign up fee per person. Husain and I raced home to ask Abu Shante for the seed money to begin our basketball career. When we arrived home, our front door was wide open. Someone had broken into our house while we were away and stole our valuables. When our parents returned home, we didn't have the heart to ask for the 40 dollars needed to join the basketball team.

That ended our affinity for basketball, but propelled us towards football.

5
FOOTBALL BOOTY

After watching Abbas play a supporting role on a football team that lost in the championship game, Husain's and my interest in football piqued.

"Abu Shante?" I asked.

"Yeah soldier?"

"Can Husain and I play football next year?"

"Oh, so now you want to play?"

"Yes sir."

"What made you change your mind?"

"I liked how much fun Abbas was having."

"Oh yeah? What else?"

"I liked the jerseys, the trophies, the pizza parties, and the banquet."

"Oh. So now you see a different side of football?"

"Yes sir."

"See, it's more than just hitting and getting hit. Football is a teacher."

"A teacher?"

"Umm hmm. Football teaches a number of things like toughness, teamwork, and sportsmanship."

"I see...but I want to win. I want a trophy, and I want to score touchdowns."

"Haha, you can win and score touchdowns, but you have to learn to lose too."

"But I don't like to lose."

"No one likes to lose, but it's a part of the game. Losing and injuries."

"I don't want to lose or get hurt."

"It's football son. You're going to do both, but remember this: don't let anyone see you cry after a loss, and don't let anyone carry you off the field after being hurt."

19

"Yes sir."

"Alright, let's shake on it—you're giving me your word right?"

"Yes sir."

"And you're going to do your absolute best?"

"Yes sir."

"Alright, you can play."

And with that, I returned to the city where I first met Abu Shante; Chino, CA.

We held our practices for Chino Pop Warner, five minutes from the prison. Under the lights, I learned valuable lessons from the game of football but also from Abu Shante aka Brother Yusuf and Coach Yusuf. He wore different hats, but he was always there to support me, Abbas, and Husain. He helped us go from having a football phobia to being football fanatics. We needed football, and it appeared as though football needed us. Our rise in the game of football was not without its struggles and obstacles; yet Abu Shante stayed the course and led us from Pop Warner, to high school, and on to college.

Football became the one thing that brought a father and his sons together.

6

THE BIRTH OF AN NFL CAREER

"Scoot over!"
"What?"
"I said scoot over!"
"Who are you?"
"I'm Hamza Abdullah, who are you?"
"I'm Madrigal."
"Well, Madrigal, why are you so close to me?"
"Because there's no room in here."
"Yes, there is. Scoot over."
"I can't, I'm squished."
"Squished?"
"Yeah, someone's on the other side of me."
"Well, tell them to scoot over."
"Hey you, scoot over," Madrigal yelled.
"I can't scoot over, and why are you yelling at me?"
"Because Hamza's telling me to scoot over, but I can't. You're in the way." Madrigal said.
"Who's Hamza?"
"I'm Hamza. Who are you?"
"I'm Ryan. I don't appreciate you guys yelling at me."
"Well, I don't appreciate you guys being so close to me." I said, annoyance in my tone.
"We have no choice, there are millions of us in here." Ryan revealed.
"Millions? Where are we?" I asked
"We're in the football testes. Pee Wee Football." Ryan said.
"The football testes?" Madrigal inquired.

21

"Yeah. This is the starting place for everyone who wants to go to the National Football League." Ryan declared.

"How many get to go?" I asked.

"One." Ryan stated.

"One?" Madrigal and I asked in unison.

"Yep. One," Ryan said proudly; "and I'm going to be that one."

"~~Bullshit~~," exclaimed Madrigal, "I'll be that one."

"Well, I don't know who'll be that one to make it to the NFL, but I'm about to get to work." I stated with a hint of shaky confidence, "But may the best man win."

My introduction to football was standard amongst most NFL Players. We get our start in Pee Wee football, or the football testes. We begin as a single cell trying to defy the odds. We aspire to be that one cell that reaches the NFL's fallopian tube. We understand it won't be easy. We contend with the other millions of cells who also covet the inner lining of a womb's walls. When the whistle is blown on our first competitive youth football game, ejaculation has started, and the race is on. We sprint to be that chosen one.

The first test is the cervix, or high school football. As we squeeze our way to the top of the tract, we begin to notice millions of our comrades begin to falter and fall behind. The transition from youth league to high school is a massive leap. There are no longer volunteer coaches, team moms, and post-game pizza parties regardless of the game's outcome. It's all about winning now.

After high school is Uterus University, or college football. When we make it to the uterus, we notice the millions of aspiring cells have dwindled to just thousands. Still a large number, but we can't worry about those cells. We have to stay focused on the task at hand. We have to keep swimming. We begin to exercise habitually. We believe lifting weights and taking supplements will aid us in our ascent to the fallopian tubes ampulla region—otherwise known as the NFL Draft.

We enter the final stage of the tube in search of the egg, football's Holy Grail. The egg is where security, comfort, and nourishment happen. We set our sights on the egg, praying our name is the one that's called to fertilize and become one with the egg.

"With the two hundred thirty-first pick in the 2005 NFL Draft, the Tampa Bay Buccaneers select: Hamza Abdullah, Defensive Back from Washington State University."

I won.

After our victory lap we are indoctrinated on the way of the womb. The NFL's womb. As long as we adhere to this specific policy, our time in the womb will be pleasant. Veer too far right or left, and a miscarriage will be the consequence. When we begin our embryonic stage of the NFL, we develop a sturdy capsule around us—the NFL Shield.

The Shield brings pelf, privilege, and protection. The NFL must protect their investment while making sure the embryo is carried to term. The average term of an NFL pregnancy is three-and-a-half years.

Just like the pregnancy cycle of a human being, there are certain dangers that accompany an embryo that doesn't make it to term as well as if it's carried passed the term. For embryos that don't make it to term in the NFL womb, they will be without health care and benefits after birth. For the embryos that occupy the womb for longer than the term allows, they are subjected to illusionary hopes. They will grow bigger and fatter in the womb, thinking they'll never have to leave. To them, birth is an urban legend.

Shortly after their inception into the womb, the placenta is grown.
The placenta is equipped with agents, financial advisors, managers, and personal assistants to ensure the proper development of this new being. The placenta is directly connected from player to the NFL through an umbilical cord. The umbilical cord provides nutrients from the NFL to its newest offspring, and discards the waste. Legal issues, bad relationships, and old neighborhoods are among the many wastes being removed through the umbilical cord.

Life is good inside the womb.

While inside the womb, we are unaware of the realities of the world. The NFL goes to great lengths to protect its embryo from the important issues that would take the focus of the embryo away from the utopia it experiences.

Politics, religion, war, violence, and death have no business entering the womb. Layer after layer protects the embryo from the outside world.

My time in the womb lasted seven years. Seven years of comfort and protection. Then all of a sudden, my world around me began to tremble. The contractions began when I least expected it.

"Hey Hamza, come up and see me when you're done down here."
"Of course, Coach." I nonchalantly responded.
After cleaning my locker out, I headed upstairs to my coach's office.

"Now Hamza, you've done a remarkable job for us this season."
"Thank you, Coach."
"You've done everything we've asked you to do and more."
"I've tried my hardest."
"You stayed healthy all year and anchored our Special Teams unit."
"Yes, sir. I wanted to make my mark on this team wherever you needed me."
"...And you did. We talked about you replacing last year's Special Teams captain, and you filled the role valiantly."
"Thank you, Coach."
"You were a leader in the locker room, and you stepped up as a leader on the team."
"Like I said, Coach, wherever you needed me, I was going to be there."
"I know. I have to admit something to you," reluctance in his tone.
"What's that, Coach?" I eagerly anticipated his words.
"When our starting safety got hurt, I should have put you into the lineup."

As a player, these type of statements from coaches make our blood boil. We abide by the rules, we do the dirty work, we keep our mouths shut, and we work hard with the expectation that when it's our turn to shine, we get to shine. So when the opportunity comes and we don't get to shine—after paying our dues—we are upset.

"Coach, I'm going to be honest. I don't know what to say to that."
"I know. I know it's not something you want to hear, but it's the truth and I owe you that."
"It's a little late for that."
"I apologize, Hamza. I really do."
"So what do I have to do to make sure I'm not overlooked again?"
"Honestly, Hamza? Nothing. With other players, I can tell them to go home and work on this or work on that, but for you, I can't."

Another statement that I've heard my entire career. I'm trying to be cordial, but I've had enough of the politics. I'm a football player and I want to play football.

"So what am I supposed to do now?"
"Well, hopefully we'll bring you back and give you an opportunity to compete for the starting job. That's if you want to come back."
"Coach, I just want to play. I miss playing on Defense. I miss playing when it counts. I miss playing football."
"I'm sure you do, and all I can say is I want you back."
"What does that mean?"
"Well, from the coaches' perspective, we want you here, but as you know, the other side of the building is an entity of its own."
"The Front Office?"
"Yeah. We just tell them who we want back and they determine if the economics coincide with that plan."
"All right."
"What year is this for you Hamza?"
"I just finished my seventh year, Coach."
"Well, you know how this process works. You're a veteran with a good contract; I'll be surprised if you're not back next year."
"We'll see...Thank you for your time, Coach."
"Thank you, Hamza. It really was a pleasure coaching you. All the best."
"Thanks, Coach."

The contractions began and I began to slide downward. The contractions in the NFL usually consists of outside pressures, injuries, a first rounder drafted at your position, a new coaching staff, or an expensive contract.

The first sign of change is usually a players thirtieth birthday. That's when his water breaks. It's not a matter of *if* birth will happen, but *when* it will happen.

From that point on, the fully formed fetus is on the way out. Our descent into real life takes on a slow, careful, methodical transition. We come out head first to a different type of light. Our vision is not quite ready for this new world, so we close our eyes as we are flushed out of the womb. When we are halfway out of the womb, we are abruptly snatched out. We, along with our placenta, are promptly discarded. Our lockers are swiftly cleaned out, name plate removed, and any remnants of our existence are thrown into a garbage bag. Our umbilical cord is cut, and that's the last time we receive proper nutrients.

An abrupt end to what we once assumed was our "happily ever after."

The NFL prepares the womb for another unsuspecting embryo. With every baby born by the NFL, the host NFL becomes stronger, wealthier, and more powerful. The NFL cuts its ties, leaves the being in the wilderness to fend for itself, and searches for the next sperm cell to cultivate and grow.

The doctor in a human birth has two patients, the mother and child. It is the doctor's responsibility to make sure both patients have the best care. In the instance of an NFL birth, the player doesn't have the same insurance the NFL has—so the player will not be taken care of.

The NFL walks away healthy, but the child is left to mixed results. What's needed in that delivery room is a nurse. That nurse is the other former players; the players who not long before were also being birthed after an NFL career. The nurse's responsibility is the overall care and development of this NFL infant until that infant can grow to take care of himself. The NFL Alumni Association and National Football League Players Association can act as midwives to check in after the baby's birth to make sure he is on track to becoming a healthy contributor to society.

These infants, when properly looked after with great pediatric care, can move on to become some of the most influential people in our society. It's a shame that some will die of Sudden Infant Death Syndrome before ever reaching their full potential.

It's perceived that many NFL players—after they leave the NFL—have a tough time adjusting to life after football, yet there has been little done to alleviate the problem. I aim to see if this is true, and if so, to find a cure for SIDS in NFL players and to help put an end to players going broke, getting divorces, or committing suicide.

I'll have to go back where it all started...

7
"POPS" WARNER

It was my first year playing football and I just had a bad practice. A practice where I dropped a ball and missed a tackle. I sat silently, wishing I were in bed. I'd never make it to the NFL playing like that. I was riding shotgun with Abu Shante. He sensed my defeatist attitude during our ride and wasn't going to allow me to be down on myself.

"What's going on soldier?"
"Nothing."
"It doesn't seem like nothing."
"I'm just thinking."
"Well, don't think too hard. It's just a game."
"Yes, sir."
"One day you're going to get paid to play this game."
"You think so?"
"I know so. One day, they're going to pay you to stay in shape."
"*In shaa Allah*...God willing."
"*In shaa Allah*. Just keep working out and working hard."
"Yes, sir."

I felt a sense of power and purpose. My pops believed in me. That was all I needed. I wouldn't let him down. I was going to work harder than anyone else. I appreciated those words from my dad. I needed a pick-me-up, and he delivered. He was not about to let me mope.

"Hamza, reach over and hand me that tape."
"This one?"

"Yeah. Let's pop this in."
I wondered what was on the tape. I sat up in anticipation of the message.

"You don't know nothing about this." My dad teased.
"About what?" I inquired.

I hear a drum then horns begin playing a rhythmic melody: Boom, Boom, Boom, Psssh. Doom doom doom, doo doo doo doo doo—doo doo doo. Pop Pop Pop Pop Pop—Pop. Doom doom doom, doo doo doo doo doo— doo doo doo. Pop Pop Pop Pop Pop—Pop.

I was thinking, what is this? Before I could say anything, Abu Shante turned to me and began singing with the lead singer.

"Step right up
 Hurry, hurry,
 Before the show begins..."

"Where is this going?" I chuckled.

I found it comical my dad could sing. The song he was singing was really smooth. I began to smile and nod my head while listening to my pops. He continued singing.

"So let the sideshow begin,
Hurry, Hurry, step right on in
Can't afford to pass it by,
Guaranteed to make you cry..."

I caught on quickly. My dad was looking for me to join in the duet, so I relaxed and began singing.

"Let the sideshow begin..."

My dad nodded in affirmation and sang louder. He was proud of me and I was proud of him. I was proud of him for opening up to me and showing rare emotion. He was a tough man with tough hands. Hands that weren't known for pats on the back. I soaked in the moment. It was a classic moment that sons long to have with their fathers. A moment where we've been accepted. My dad made a promise to me that if I continued to work, I would get paid to play football. He also subtly taught me to let bad practices or games roll off my back. Whenever I would feel down, all I needed was to put on that Blue Magic tape. Thank you, Abu Shante. Let the sideshow begin.

8

COMBINE CORRECTIONAL FACILITY

"You have been invited to the 2005 NFL Combine in Indianapolis, Indiana."

I never really grasped the fact that I would be an NFL Player until the spring of 2005, when a certified letter came in the mail. It was from the league office inviting me to its annual collegiate combine. I was ecstatic. It was a milestone achievement for an aspiring professional football player. I assumed I would be integrated into NFL culture with the protection of a shepherd.

I was sadly mistaken.

Upon my arrival in Indianapolis, I—along with six other naive prospects— was herded into a white cargo van. The van looked as though it would be used for a bank robbery and set on fire later in the day. There were no smiles, handshakes, or salutations exchanged between anyone in the van. The mood was somber, as though we were going to an execution. An execution of our football careers. We arrived at the hotel next to the stadium and unloaded like a chain gang. We were all branded like cattle and shown to our cells.

I was "DB 22." Defensive Back Number 22. Hamza Abdullah no longer existed. I was poked, prodded, and carefully examined everywhere I went. The excitement of joining the National Football League dissipated. I wanted to go home, but I was sentenced to three days in the NFL's version of Basic Training. Before leaving Indianapolis, I piled all the Combine

30

material in a corner and wished it would internally combust. I wanted it gone. The clothes, the memories, and the performance.

My testing numbers weren't what I had expected them to be, and I attributed it to the environment. It didn't seem like a nurturing environment that bred success.

It was more of a meat market where we were measured, weighed, and evaluated purely on our physical appearance. We were pieces of meat sold to the highest bidder.

It was a modern day slave trade.

I couldn't say how I felt then, because it would have been ignored. I was no Nat Turner, more Ike Turner. I became abusive due to the stress, strain, and trauma I endured. Not physically, but emotionally and verbally I took it out on those around me who loved me. My wife caught the brunt of it. For seven years she saw me battle with my soul over the injustices of the NFL. I knew one day I would have to stand up and say something.

9

DRAFT DOUBT

The NFL Draft was days away, and I went from a confident prospect to a nervous wreck. I began to second guess myself, my ability, and my future. What if I didn't get drafted? What if I couldn't play at that level? What would I do if I couldn't go to the NFL? If I'm not Hamza the football player, who would I be? All of these questions were swirling through my head as I spoke to my future wife.

I met Alexa a year earlier, and we were in the beginning stages of preparation for marriage. I had met Alexa's family, but she had yet to meet mine. The NFL Draft weekend made for a perfect time. She picked out new clothes, new shoes, and a new hairstyle. She was all ready to meet the Abdullahs.

"I just don't think it's a good idea," reluctancy in my tone.
"It was a good idea a week ago." Alexa stated.
"I know, but...but..."
"Why don't you want me to meet your family?"
"I do. I just don't think this is a good time."
"I don't get it, Hamza. Last week you wanted me to go, now you don't. Why not?"
"I just don't know if I'm going to get drafted."
"You're going to get drafted. You're one of the best players in the nation and you had a great workout."
"I know, but you never know. I would hate for you to fly all the way to California and I don't get drafted."
"Hamza. Regardless of what happens, God has a plan for you. Don't worry about it. Everything will work out. I just want to be with you to support you, and I want to meet your family."

32

"I know you want to support me, but..."

"Fine, Hamza, I won't argue with you. If that's what you want..."

"It is. I'm sorry Alexa. God willing, it will be better after this is all done."

I felt Alexa's anger, but I didn't want to disappoint her. How embarrassing would it be to bring my wife-to-be to my parents' house to celebrate me going to the NFL, and I end up not going to the NFL? It was my decision, and it was a bad decision. I should have let her be there for me.

My family and I woke up early Sunday morning for the second day of the NFL Draft. Back then, the Draft was held on two consecutive days. Rounds one through three were on Saturday and rounds four through seven were on Sunday. Each round consisted of anywhere between 32 and 40 picks.

Two hundred and fifty-five picks in total.

I was so nervous, I didn't eat or drink a thing. My stomach was tied up in knots. Then the draft started. The first player taken was Sean Considine, a defensive back from the University of Iowa. Maybe this was a sign that they would start drafting DB's. The next pick was also a defensive back, Antonio Perkins from the University of Oklahoma. I played against him in the Rose Bowl.

The next pick was also a defensive back, Travis Daniels from Louisiana State University. I would end up playing with him in Cleveland. Four picks later, my training partner, friend and fellow DB Vincent Fuller was drafted. Seven picks later, another DB. Then another and another. The fourth round was the round of DB's.

I just knew I was going to get picked. My stomach began to ease up and my spirits lifted. I started talking, engaging more with my family, telling jokes, smiling and anticipating a phone call from my new team. As I sat in the living room of my parents' home, the fourth round came to a close. No sign of Hamza Abdullah.

Then the fifth round came and went faster than a Deion Sanders forty yard dash. No sign of Hamza Abdullah.

Six picks into the sixth round, one of my buddies from our college all-star game, Chris Harris, defensive back from Louisiana-Monroe, was selected.

He earned it. It always felt good when someone I knew got picked, because I know what waiting feels like. It's not easy.

Chris would go on to an All-Pro career with the Chicago Bears and Carolina Panthers. Seven picks after Chris another one of my training partners and DB's, C.C. Brown from Louisiana-Lafayette, was taken. I knew my name was coming up soon. I was right. Twenty picks after C.C. was taken, the Dallas Cowboys were on the clock.

My phone rang.

"*Assalamu Alaikum*," I said.
"Hey. Is this Hamza Abdullah?"
"Yes sir, it is. May I ask who's speaking?"
"This is Coach Blah Blah, with the Dallas Cowboys."
"Hey Coach, how are you?"
"I'm great. Just checking in with you, seeing if you want to be a Dallas Cowboy?"

I began to sweat, a lump formed in my throat and I couldn't speak. I began to get choked up. My family stood up and gathered around me.

I knew this was it. I was going to be a Dallas Cowboy. The coach didn't know if I was still there.

"Hamza, you still there?"
"Yes, sir."
"Okay Hamza, we have two picks back to back here, so I'm not sure which one we'll take you with."
"Coach as long as you take me, it doesn't matter which one it is."

With the phone still to my ear, I hear: "The pick is in." I inch up closer to the television expecting to see my name, but instead I see:

"With the two hundred and eighth pick in the 2005 NFL Draft, the Dallas Cowboys select: Justin Beriault, Defensive Back from Ball State."

What?
I look at the phone. The Coach isn't speaking and neither am I. I think to myself that maybe they're drafting two defensive backs. Hey, that's okay, I'll go and compete to the best of my ability. With the phone still to my

ear, I hear: "The pick is in." I again inch up closer to the television, just to make sure there aren't any typos this time. It happens again:

"With the two hundred and ninth pick in the 2005 NFL Draft, the Dallas Cowboys select: Rob Petitti, Tackle from the University of Pittsburgh."

I stare at my phone. I stretch it out at arm's length still looking at the display. The call hadn't dropped, the coach was still on the line. I hung up the phone. My family backed away from me not wanting to catch an errant elbow. I hung my head knowing that was my only chance. I thought to myself, who would do a thing like that? What a cruel joke to play on a young college kid trying to achieve his dream. I began to lie to myself. I told myself I didn't want to play for the Cowboys anyway.

My family began to sense the intense pressure I was feeling, so they felt leaving would alleviate that pressure. Everyone, except my older brother Abbas, left the house. Abbas sat with me as the sixth round came to a close. Again, no sign of Hamza Abdullah.

Now here we were in the seventh and final round of the NFL Draft. My phone began to ring off the hook. Teams began to try to fill their roster with guys that didn't get drafted. If I wasn't drafted, I would be a free agent, which meant I could pick the team I went to, but I wouldn't get as much guaranteed money as a draft pick. I got calls from St. Louis, Pittsburgh, and Arizona.

They told me that if I didn't get picked, they would love to have me on their team. I thought it was odd, because all of these teams still had picks in the seventh round. If they really wanted me, they'd pick me. Then my phone rang.

Another unfamiliar area code, this one read 813. I picked up, trying not to get my hopes up and expecting some unknown scout on the other end to tell me they wanted me to sign there as a free agent.

"*Assalamu Alaikum.*"
"Hey. What's going on? This Hamza?"
"Yes sir, it is."
"Hamza, this is Jon Gruden, Head Coach of the Tampa Bay Buccaneers."
"Oh. Hey Coach."
"How would you like to be a Buc?"

"Are you serious? Coach, I would love it. Are you picking me?"
"Yes, sir. We're taking you right now. Here, someone wants to talk to you."

There was a pause on the line, then another voice.

"Hamza, how you doing? This is Coach Mike Tomlin. I'm your new position coach."
"I'm doing great, sir. How are you?"
"Great, now that we have you on board. Hold on, they're about to announce the pick."

I look at the television screen one more time. The draft is on commercial. During an ad for a beer sponsor, the bottom of the screen reads:

"Pick is in....With 231st pick, the Tampa Bay Buccaneers select: Hamza Abdullah {Defensive Back} Washington State University."

Tears began to rush down my face. Abbas excitedly paced and in between rubbing my shoulders and doing fist pumps like Tiger Woods at Augusta, he's also crying.

We made it.

Unlike the earlier snafu with the Cowboys, Coach Tomlin stayed on the line.

"Hamza, Congratulations."
"Thank you, Coach...Will I get a chance to compete?"
"We wouldn't have picked you if we didn't want you to compete."

With that, I was a member of the National Football League.

10

MR. ABDULLAH

Two weeks after I was drafted into the NFL, I sat in the airport lounge at Seattle-Tacoma International airport awaiting a flight to Tampa.

I had never been to Florida, but I had always wanted to go.

PA Announcer

"Now boarding flight 770—Nonstop from Seattle to Tampa Bay"

I checked to see if that was my flight, and it was, so I walked around until I thought I found the assigned gate.

"Excuse me. Excuse me, Miss?"
"Yes, sir?"
"Sir?" I chuckled, not used to being addressed as a sir. "Yes, ma'am, I wanted to make sure I was in the right place."
"Let me see," she cheerfully responded while glancing at my ticket. "Yes sir, Mr. Abdullah, you're in the right place."

This wasn't my first time on an airplane, but it was my first time being treated so well.

"Mr. Abdullah, you can go ahead and board the plane."
"But no one else has boarded."
"They'll board later. You have priority access, so you get to board first."

"Okay, cool. I've never had that. Thank you."

As I walked to the gate to board, I noticed the other passengers analyzing me. I wasn't sure whether I had done something wrong, so I hesitantly approached the woman attending the gate.

"Come on."
"Me?"
"Yes, sir. I saw you talking to Molly, so you're clear to board."
"Okay."

"Your ticket, please." She grabbed my ticket and glanced at it with a look of surprise. She looked back at me with a seductive smile and said, "Enjoy your flight."

"Thank you," I muttered. I wasn't sure of the source of all this unwanted attention.

Walking down the breezeway towards the plane, I contemplated the reason for the attention. Maybe it was the book I was holding, *The Autobiography of Malcolm X*? Maybe it was the Washington State University hat I was wearing? Whatever it was, I wanted to get to the bottom of it.

As I approached the cabin door, I was again met by a smiling woman.

"Good morning, sir."
"Good morning."
"If I may be of any assistance, please don't hesitate to ask."
"Thank you."

I looked at my ticket for my seat assignment, 6C. I walked down the aisle but couldn't find my seat. Perplexed, I turned to the flight attendant to ask for help.

"Excuse me. Excuse me, Ms? I can't seem to find my seat."
"Let me see your ticket."
"Yes, ma'am, here it is," I said, removing the ticket from my book.
"Well, you're not going to find your seat back here, Mr. Abdullah," she said with a smirk.
"Why not?" I asked with genuine concern in my voice.
"Because this is the main cabin, and you're seated in first class."
"First Class what?"

38

"Don't be silly," she said giggling. "Here, I'll show you to your seat."

"Okay," I said glancing at my ticket again.

"Here you are, Mr. Abdullah. Nancy will be taking care of you today. Enjoy your flight," she said with a sly grin.

As I sat down in the love seat, I couldn't help but smile. Was this how NFL players traveled? Was this why everyone shot me covetous looks? Why would they be jealous of me? I'm only 21 years old, and this is my first time flying First Class.

I said a prayer thanking God for this experience. I was thankful to the Buccaneers organization and to the NFL. I was going to enjoy this flight and my time in the NFL.

11
WELCOME TO THE NFL

Today is my twenty-second birthday, my future wife is in town, and it's game day. The Tampa Bay Buccaneers are hosting the Jacksonville Jaguars in the second preseason game. There are only four preseason games, so I don't have much time to show I can play with the big boys.

The first preseason game was okay, but I didn't do anything to stand out. Preseason is all about young players standing out. I prayed before I put on my uniform, I prayed before I left the locker room, and I prayed before I stepped onto the field.

"Black 16. Blaaaack 16. Set hut. Hut."

As the quarterback began his cadence, I got into position. I was the deep safety. The last line of defense. If the offense got behind me, it would be a touchdown. My job was to protect the defense. Whether the offense chose to run or pass, I had to make a stand. The quarterback's first cadence was a dummy call. It was meant to see where the defense would align and if any extra defenders were blitzing.

"Blue 13. Bluuuuue 13. Set hut. Hut."

The center snapped the ball to the quarterback, and he turned around to give the ball to the running back. I began to backpedal, just in case it was a trick. Quarterbacks at this level are very persuasive when it comes to their mechanics. They make the pass plays and the run plays look exactly the same. I stayed in my back pedal as I looked at the two wide receivers to my left running full speed. That's a dead giveaway that the play is a pass. If it's a run play, the wide receivers would block the defender in front of them. On a pass, they're trying to run away from the guy in front of them.

It was a play-action. I was right. Fake the run, throw the pass.

The quarterback was surveying the field and he saw me in the middle of the field. Then he glanced at his slot receiver, the receiver closest to me. The receiver ran a good route and was running at an angle toward the top corner of the field. His defender must have slipped or fell for the run fake, because he was nowhere in sight.

I began to weave towards the unaccompanied receiver, not yet committing just in case there was another receiver to my right running free. The quarterback saw the receiver running wide open and he tilted his shoulder up and prepared to launch. I looked at the receiver running away and hightailed it to the meeting point. The meeting point of the wide receiver, the ball, and me.

As I closed in on the receiver, I imagined reaching my hand in after he caught the ball to cause an incompletion, but as I got closer, I realized I may be able to prevent him from catching the ball by knocking it down before it got to him. Then I closed in and realized I was the first one to the meeting point. Now was the time to stand out. I reached out like Willie Mays catching a pop fly. I snatched the ball away from the receiver.

"Interception! Buccaneers!" The PA announcer shouted.

I ran back to the home sideline where the defensive captain of the Buccaneers, Shelton Quarles, greeted me with a chest bump. He jumped, but I really jumped. I jumped over him. My teammates waited for me to land, then mobbed me.

I was one of them now.

Until that point I had been teetering on the brink of being cut. At least, that's what I thought. I hadn't done anything to make the coaches remember me. Now, they'll remember me. I belonged.

Now I could take the next step with my future wife. I was certainly going to make the team now. I'd have a great paying job, we could get a house, and I could buy a new car. I'd have the stability I was looking for before bringing Alexa along for the NFL ride.

Yes. This is the best birthday present a man could ask for. An interception, a job, and a wife. Life was looking up. Happy Birthday to me.

12

PINKY SWEAR

I played well in the fourth and final preseason game against the Houston Texans but it wasn't enough. The day after the game I was called into the coach's office and asked to "bring my playbook." I was surprised because I put together a solid performance in the final two preseason games. Unfortunately it didn't matter. The Buccaneers were deep at the safety position and I found myself on the outside looking in. I didn't have any hard feelings toward the team, I was thankful they took a chance and drafted me. I figured I'd be fine because I had just signed a contract. I'll at least have money while I wait for my next team to call.

At least that's what I thought.

In the NFL we don't sign contracts. We sign promissory notes, with people whose fingers are crossed behind their backs. The second a player is injured or not playing up to the level the owner deems necessary to justify the contract, that player's contract is ripped up. The player is released, and so are the fingers behind the owners back. The owner never has to hear from said player again. Just years earlier, that player made headlines because his team "GAVE" him an exorbitant amount of money. Now, just a few years removed, this player finds himself in the back pages of the newspaper under the column named, "Transactions."

The NFL is widely considered the most dangerous of the four major American sports. The National Hockey League, Major League Baseball, National Basketball Association and the NFL make up the four major American sports. Yet, the NFL is the only sport without guaranteed

43

contracts. How is this legal? A contract, as is defined in the Webster's Dictionary, reads as such:

Contract 1) n. an agreement between two or more people for doing something, esp. one formally set forth in writing and enforceable by law.

By law.

By Law sticks out like a sore thumb. How is it permissible for one party of the contract, the NFL, to be able to waffle, while the other party, the player, must hold firmly to the contracts stipulations? I, like 99 percent of America, thought when a player signs an NFL contract, he has "made it."

My first contract with the Buccaneers was for five years and $1.3 million dollars. I was on top of the world. My world was not that tall, because it didn't take long to come back down to the ground floor.
I saw $42,000 Dollars of the $1.3 million dollars that I signed for.

I didn't understand it. At least give me that point three of the 1.3.
Unfortunately, we're talking about the NFL. The NFL doesn't "GIVE" anyone anything. I looked at my contract, and at the top of the contract it stated:

> 1.   TERM. This contract covers 5 football season(s), and will begin on the date of execution or <u>May 1, 2005</u>, whichever is later, and end on <u>February 28, 2010</u>, unless extended, TERMINATED, or renewed as specified elsewhere in this contract.

Terminated.

That was me. I was a termite eating away at the wood of the famed One Buc Place. The piece of crap trailers the Buccaneers called a Facility. The Buccaneers called in the terminators who sprayed me and left me for dead. As I lay on my back with my pads on, I wondered how this could happen. How could they tell my parents and the rest of America I was a millionaire, when the reality was, I was barely a thousandaire.

After paying my debts and loans and divvying out gifts for my family, I had $10,000 dollars to my name. It was more money than I ever had, but it was very different from the amount I assumed I was getting. This was not the first time and wouldn't be the last time that I would assume the NFL had my best interest at heart.

13

WORKOUTS WITH WIFEY

My stay in Tampa Bay was short. I signed a five year deal but only stayed five months. As I boarded the flight from Tampa back to Seattle, I glanced at the ticket to see my seat assignment: 26E.

I was back where I belonged. The way back. In the middle seat—of the last row—in a seat that didn't recline. Luckily the flight was only six hours.

I thought about my Dad and letting him down. How would I tell him I was no longer an NFL player? I slipped on my headphones trying not to think about it. The first song that played was a classic, sung by Deniece Williams:

"Silly of me to think that you
  could ever really want me too..."

She was speaking directly to my soul.

"You're just a lover out to score
  I know that I should be looking for more
  What could it be in you I see..."

Why do I love the NFL so much? Why did I love this game? I loved everything about it until I couldn't play it anymore.

"Oh, Love
  Oh, Love

Stop making a fool of me..."

That's exactly what I looked like right then—a damn fool. I knew people were going to ask what happened and how I got cut, but I figured I'd make something up and tell them they still wanted me. Deniece must have known what I was plotting.

"And foolish of me to tell them all
 That every night and day you call
 When you could care less..."

I needed someone that cared.

I needed Alexa. She was finishing up her senior year at Washington State. I knew it was time for me to go home. Home was where my heart was, but it wasn't where my work was. I fell into a depressive stupor after not being called by another NFL team.

After weeks of sitting around my college apartment I started planning for life after football. I began studying for the West-B test and researched local teaching and coaching positions. If I wanted to get married, I needed a stable career. The NFL wasn't it.

Alexa was not going to let me use her as a scapegoat to being a quitter. One day she called me after class to stress this point.

"Hamza?"
"*Assalamu Alaikum*?"
"Hamza, you know it's me."
"Yes, I do, but this is how I answer my phone, regardless of who's calling."
"...But, I'm not Muslim."
"That's okay."
"Can't you just say hello when you know it's me?"
"Why would I want to tell you hell is low, when I can give you a peaceful greeting?"
"Whatever you say, Hamza."
I snickered...

"What are you doing right now?"
"Nothing. Just looking some stuff up."
"What kind of stuff?" Alexa asked curiously.
"I'm looking for job openings."

"What kind of job?"

"A high school basketball coach."

"You don't play basketball." Alexa caught herself from laughing out loud.

"I can learn." I retorted.

"So what about the NFL?"

"I haven't heard from them. I can't just sit around waiting for them to call."

"You can't just sit around—period."

"You're right."

"You can be working out preparing for when the NFL *does* call."

"How do you know they will call?"

"I don't know, but I have faith that they will."

"*In shaa Allah.*"

"What?"

"God willing."

"Oh. Yeah. God willing; but you have to be ready when they do call. God willing."

"I just don't want to be working out for no reason."

"You'll be working out for a reason, and I'll be working out with you."

"You will?"

"Yeah. I'm going to work out with you. We can start by running stadium stairs."

"Man, you're serious about this."

"I'm serious about you. I'm not going to sit by and let you give up on your future."

"Thank you, Alexa."

"That's what I'm here for. I'm done with classes, so we can go workout now."

"Right now?"

"Yep."

"All right. *In shaa Allah* I'll meet you at the stadium."

"*In shaa Allah.*"

"See, you're getting it!" I chuckled, amused that she repeated the Arabic words. "*Assalamu Alaikum.*"

"What do I say to that?"

"You say, *Wa alaikumu salam.*"

"*Wa alaikumu salaam?*"

"Yes. Isn't that better than hello?"

"It is. What does it mean again?"

"Peace be unto you."

"I like that."

"I like you."

"I bet you do."

Thanks to Alexa I didn't hang up my cleats or hang up when an NFL team did call. I found a home on the Denver Broncos roster shortly after resuming my daily workouts with Alexa.

14

DENVER

I became a man in Denver.

Denver is where I got married and had my first child, Layla. I believe a male becomes a man when he realizes his life is no longer dedicated to his own personal gain. After getting married and having a daughter I realized life wasn't all about me. A real man protects those closest to him, especially the women and children. With a wife and daughter, I was no longer earning money to better my own future but the future of my family.

Playing for the Broncos allowed me to benefit others. The Broncos organization was notorious for doing work in the community. Pat Bowlen, the longtime owner of the Denver Broncos, believed the city of Denver was one big family and the Broncos were the leaders of that family. My teammates became my brothers. John Lynch, the future Hall of Famer, along with Nick Ferguson—the best tackler I've ever seen—took me under their wings. They were the Starting safeties, leaders of the team, and leaders in the community. They showed me how to be a professional athlete in a town that loved its professional athletes. Life in Denver was simple. Play well, be visible in the community, and appreciate your position.

What I loved about Denver was the absence of classism. On other teams it was evident which players made the most money; not so on the Broncos. Our starting quarterback, Jake Plummer, drove a Honda Pilot. Our All-World cornerback, Champ Bailey, drove an SUV that could only be described as a jalopy and our head coach drove an old Mercedes in need of more than a tune-up. Here were people with a justifiable position of power and status, but they traded it in to have a position with the people. This show of humility forced me to buy into the creed of the team: WE, not me.

We were together. We were strong. We were good. We were family.

I loved my family.

I wanted to spend my entire NFL career in Denver. Denver was home—or so I thought.

The 2005 season ended in disappointment as we lost one game short of the Super Bowl. No problem, I knew we'd be back the next year, and this time we would win it.

After an unimpressive 2006 campaign where we limped to an 8-8 record, I figured the team was in for a tumultuous offseason. I'm not sure anyone could prepare for what was to come.

The ringing phone startled me awake.

I roll over in bed and glance at my cellphone:

3:47 AM

January 1, 2007

I wonder who's calling me and why it can't wait until later. I silenced the phone and rolled back over.

The phone rang again.

This time, I rolled back over, picked up the phone and answered.

"Hamza?"
"*Assalamu Alaikum*..." I said while clearing my throat.
"Hamza?"
"Yeah."
"This is Nico." Nico was the nickname given to Nick Ferguson.
"What's going on, Nico?"
"Go turn on SportsCenter." Nick said in a low tone.

"Turn on SportsCenter? Why?" I responded curiously.
"Just please. Go turn on SportsCenter." Nick said heavily.

I got out of bed and walked to the living room of my apartment. Still holding the phone to my head, I searched for the remote in the dark. I found the remote, aimed at the TV and pressed power.

For those of you just joining us, we have Breaking News into SportsCenter. Denver Broncos cornerback Darrent Williams was shot and killed in downtown Denver earlier this morning...

I sat staring at the screen. I tried to speak but I couldn't. I tried to move but I couldn't. I was frozen. A picture of Darrent was on the screen with 1982-2007 under his name. I didn't want to believe it, but I had no choice. This was my new reality. Nick had been waiting for me to come out of my haze.

"Ni-Nic-Nico..."
"I'm here."
"Nico, this isn't..."
"Yeah, Hamza...We lost D. Will."
"...But I was supposed to go..."
"I know. I was, too..."
"I just..."
"I know. It's tough. I hate to have to call you and give you this news."
"Nico. Man. I don't..."
"I'm here for you, brother."
"Did you call Fox?"
"I'm calling the guys now."
"All right."
"I'll see you in a few hours."
"Okay...Thanks, Nico."

I was devastated, as was every other member of our team. We had just played a game. Now, a few hours later, we get the news that one of our brothers was gone.

A darkness covered the Denver Broncos facility. We were ill-equipped to handle death in the NFL. No one knew what to say, what to do, or how to move forward.

So we didn't.

We stayed in the funk until February 24, when I received another call.

I answered the phone after the second ring.

"*Assalamu Alaikum.*"
"Hamza, it happened again."
"Nico? What you talking 'bout?"
"Hamza, we lost Damien."
"What do you mean? What happened?"
"He was playing basketball, then he collapsed and died."
"What?"
"Yeah. Back in St. Louis."
"Are you serious?"
"Yeah, man. I'm calling the guys now."
"I'm sorry, Nico."
"Me too."

We lost two teammates in two months. Darrent Williams and Damien Nash.

Two brothers.

Our family was vulnerable. We were in need of something or someone to help us heal. We didn't know how to address our hurt.

So we didn't.

When offseason workouts began later that year, the organization pretended like nothing happened.

Damien and Darrent's lockers were cleaned out and given to new players without any acknowledgment. The only acknowledgment came when we would break a huddle. Instead of "team," "finish" or "win," we would say D. Will's signature line, "already." That was cool, but it was surficial. There was no team meeting or group therapy to help the healing.

So we played on.

As time went on during the 2007 season, there was a silent movement to slowly move away from the tragedies by getting those most affected by the tragedies out of town. Steadily, player after player was either traded or released. Our family was breaking up. I took solace in the fact that Husain was preparing to enter into the NFL and got his shot when the Minnesota Vikings signed him as an undrafted free agent. Husain was beginning his career, while mine looked to be on the rocks.

I was one of the holdovers who made it into the 2008 season, but it wouldn't last. Before long, it was my head on the chopping block. The city I grew up in was now kicking me out on my own.

15
NO INSURANCE

I was released by the Denver Broncos after spending three and a half years there. The timing was awful, as it was week three of the regular season.

I had no desire to stick around town and sulk in the city I thought was my home. In less than a week, I packed up my two bedroom apartment, a pregnant wife and toddler daughter, and headed to Seattle. Alexa and I bought a home in Seattle the previous offseason with the hopes of it being our offseason home. It turned out, we would need it during the season as well. After just a few days, we heard from the NFL. It wasn't the notice we were hoping nor looking for.

"Hamza, can you check the mail?"
"I'll go do it right now sweetheart..."

I ran out to the mailbox, where it was filled with advertisements and a certified letter.

"Anything important?"
"I don't know. There's something from the NFL..."
"What does it say?"
"It says they're cutting our health insurance off in 30 days. How? Why?"
"Wait, let me see that."
"I don't get it."
"Neither do I. Hamza, I'm six months pregnant. If we don't have insurance...how?"

"Don't worry about it, I'm going to take care of it."

"How are you going to take care of it?"

"I have to get back on a team before they cut off our insurance."

"But what if it's not a good team, or it's far away? I don't want to be away from you right now."

"I gotta do what I gotta do, sweetheart; for you, Layla, and the baby *in shaa Allah.*"

"But I don't want you to do something you don't want to do."

"What other choice do I have, sweetheart?"

"I don't know, but can we call someone?"

"I don't know, but they're going to tell me the same thing. If I'm not on a team, I don't have health insurance."

"But this is your fourth year in the league, doesn't that count for something?"

"It should, but technically, I was released before my benefits kicked in."

"That doesn't make any sense, Hamza. What are we supposed to do? What am I supposed to do?"

"Don't worry about it sweetheart. Don't worry about it...I'll take care of it. I promise."

"Okay. I need to go lay down."

16

THE HOLY CITY OF CLEVELAND

The Cleveland Browns were the first team to offer me a contract after I left Denver. Out of the other 31 NFL cities I wanted to play in, Cleveland probably wasn't in the top 30. Before signing with the Browns, I didn't have much thought on the city of Cleveland. I arrived in a bad mood that only got worse.

Not only was I away from my pregnant wife and baby girl, my salary was nearly cut in half. I thought it couldn't get worse, but it did.

I didn't appear in one regular season contest for the Browns. No family, no friends, no football. I was all alone in the "Mistake by the Lake." I started losing my way. I stopped putting my energy and effort into being the best person, the best player, and the best family man I could be. I stopped talking to Alexa, my siblings, and my friends. I started staying out late, showing up late, and drinking alcohol. I could no longer identify the man in the mirror. I curled up in the corner of my hotel room, and I began to cry. I didn't know what was going to happen next. I was on a path to lose Alexa, my career, and my life.

My mother must have had her antennas up because at that moment she called me.

"Assalamu Alaikum."
"Wa alaikumu salam, Hamza, how are you?"
"I'm okay."
"Okay? Are you sure?"

56

"Yes, I'm fine."

"Well, you don't sound fine."

"I'm all right, Ummie."

"Well, I was just checking on you to make sure you were doing okay. We miss you."

"I'm fine, and I miss you, too."

"Well, I'm not going to take too much of your time."

"Okay."

"Hamza?"

"Yes, Ma'am?"

"Did you find the Mosque?"

"No, I couldn't find it."

"Well, you need to go find it. Now."

"Ummie, I'll..."

"No, Hamza. Go find the Mosque now."

"Yes, Ma'am."

"*Assalamu Alaikum.*"

"*Wa alaikumu salam.*"

I hung up the phone and went downstairs to the concierge to get directions to the nearest Mosque. They printed up a map and directions to the Islamic Center of Cleveland.

I jumped in my rental car and headed towards 6055 W 130th St., Cleveland, OH 44130.

I tried to find the Mosque when I first arrived in Cleveland, to no avail. I told my mother I would try again, so I did. It was the early evening and close to our *Maghrib*, or sunset prayer.

I drove down 130th St., but couldn't find it again. I turned around and again searched for the Mosque. I still couldn't find it. I looked at the map again and the map showed that it was situated somewhere between the main streets Pearl Rd and Snow Rd. I thought this couldn't be right because I had just driven north and south, looking in both directions and couldn't find it. This time I went one block north to Brookpark Rd. I told myself I'm going to go slow and find the Mosque. After crossing Snow Rd, I slowed my car looking in both directions. I began having a discussion with myself.

"Man, I'm just going to go back to the hotel."

"Nah, you can't do that. You promised Ummie you'd find the Mosque."
"I know, but I've tried and it ain't here."
"It's right here on the map."
"Well, it ain't here on the street."
"Just look again, fool."
"All I see is trees."
"Me too...but isn't that a driveway right there?"
"Wait, let me see…"

As I looked past the driveway, I saw the biggest Mosque I had ever seen in my life. My heart dropped.

I've driven up and down this street, and I'd never seen this beautiful place before. The Mosque was a spectacular blue and white striped building equipped with a golden dome. The minarets rose high into the sky, distinguishing itself from an ordinary building. I pulled into the driveway and slowly made my way to the entrance. I was greeted by a middle aged man who looked to be of Indonesian descent.

"*Assalamu Alaikum.*" The brother greeted me.
"*Wa alaikumu salam.*"
"How are you, young brother?"
"I'm fine, thank you for asking. How are you?"
"Alhamdulillah, All praises are due to the Most High."
"Alhamdulillah."
"You're new here?"
"Yes sir, I am."
"Welcome. You can wash up over there, and we'll be praying in about 10 minutes."
"Thank you, brother..."
"Abdur-Rahman. My name is Brother Abdur-Rahman."
"Thank you, Brother Abdur-Rahman. My name is Hamza."
"*MashaAllah*, Hamza. Such a strong name."
"*MashaAllah...*"
"Go ahead and make *wudu*, and I'll see you soon. I have to give the *Azan*."
"Of course. Thank you again."
"*Assalamu Alaikum*"
"*Wa alaikumu salam*"

The Mosque saved my life. Brother Abdur-Rahman saved my life. My mother saved my life.

I was spiraling out of control before being ingratiated into the Muslim community of Cleveland. I had lost my religion and my way of life. Thanks to that visit to the mosque, my sense of purpose was returned.

I stopped drinking, I stopped isolating myself, and I started praying.

After Alexa gave birth to our second child, a boy we named Aqil, she joined me in Cleveland. I began to see Cleveland not for what it wasn't, but for what it was. It was a hard working city, with hard working people. I admired the fact that most people cut their own lawns—many of them women.

They were honest and surprisingly cordial. You were either with them or against them. I started as an outsider but became a Clevelander. I enjoyed my time in Cleveland but I knew I would be leaving soon. I played well during the preseason, but I was again left on the outside looking in.

After I was released by the Browns at the start of the 2009 season, I headed home to Seattle. I wanted to be a better Muslim, husband and father. I didn't know if football was helping me in my quest so I contemplated my future. A future I wasn't sure included football. I may have become a man in Denver, but I became a Muslim in Cleveland.

17
THE CALL

I went home on a mission to better myself. I began reading self-development books and religious books. I created a schedule and began teaching myself. I read The Bible and The Qur'an, and part of The Torah. I was rebuilding myself brick by brick. Alexa saw the maturation in me, but she didn't want me to give up on football.

"Hamza."

"Yeah, sweetheart?"

"How's your reading going?"

"*Alhamdulillah*, it's going great. There's so much I didn't know."

"There's so much we don't know."

"You're right."

"I'm glad you're making an effort to better yourself. I just want you to know I can tell."

"Thank you sweetheart. I just want to be better than I was."

"And you will be, *in shaa Allah*."

"Yes, *in shaa Allah*."

"So do you think you're done playing football?"

"I'm not sure...I haven't worked out in a while. I've just been trying to learn."

"Well, I appreciate you taking the steps to learn and to spend time with me and the children, but I want you to know we're going to be okay."

"I know."

"I'm saying we're going to be okay if you decide you want to still play."

"Oh...I'm just afraid I was playing for the wrong reasons. I don't want to play football if it's going to cause me to change who I am."

"I think it's all about your intentions. I know you want to play, and you're still physically able to play. I think if you're intending on playing to do good, then good will come from it."

"You're right, I do miss playing…and I do think some good could come out of me going back to play."

"Hamza, there's no monasticism in Islam."

"I know…"

"So you need to get up, get out, and get active."

"Yeah, you're right."

"You can still study and learn, but you need to apply what you're learning."

"All right, *in shaa Allah*."

"*In shaa Allah*."

I began working out again preparing for another return to the NFL. I was three months removed from playing and not sure what type of shape I was in; so I ran. I ran and ran and ran. I ran on the track, the football field, and the street. I knew it would be tough to get back into the NFL but I was determined. Running was the only thing I knew to do.

After running for weeks without an indication from NFL teams, I needed a change of scenery. The season was coming to an end and the odds of me getting signed were slim. I persuaded Alexa to take a family road trip from Seattle to Los Angeles.

She reluctantly agreed. Her main concern was our young children. We didn't know how they would deal with a long car ride but we went anyway. My younger brother Esa was visiting on his break from WSU, so he accompanied us on our trek. We left late at night in hopes that our children would sleep for the first half of the trip. We planned correctly, as they didn't wake up until our second stop for gas in southern Oregon. The ride was going smoothly as we exited the "You can't pump your own gas" state and entered into Northern California.

When we were passing the Sacramento area, my cell phone rang. I don't usually answer numbers I don't know, but I took this call. The caller ID read area code 602.

"*Assalamu Alaikum*."

"Hi, is this Hamza?"

"Yes, this is, may I ask who's speaking?"

"This is Tom, from the Arizona Cardinals."

"Oh, how are you doing?"

"I'm doing great. Look, I know it's early, but we want you to come workout for us."

"You do?"

"Yeah. We do."

"Okay, when?"

"We wanted to get you in after the game, Monday."

"Okay, that sounds good." A Monday workout meant I had a few days to prepare.

"Good, I'm glad to hear that."

"All right, I'll be ready."

"Okay, I'll put you in touch with our travel agent so she can get your flight booked."

"Thank you again."

"No, thank you. See you soon."

"Yes, sir."

Another chance. Another opportunity. Another team. A better me? Maybe. Hopefully. Ready or not, I was headed to the desert—to run in the heat.

18

RUNNING ON FUMES

T he heat was on in Arizona. The Cardinals had a great 2009 season and were preparing for another deep run into the playoffs. The season before, a well-executed two-minute drill by the Pittsburgh Steelers prevented Arizona from winning their first Super Bowl in franchise history. The team was stacked with playmakers—a balanced mixture of young talent and skilled veterans. When one of their key backups, Matt Ware, suffered a season ending knee injury, I was called. Ware was a do-it-all defensive back who could plug into any position and flourish. Not only was he a great player, he also had a big presence in the locker room.

When I showed up, everyone wondered who this new guy replacing Matt was. A quiet guy, with a strange name who wore a funny hat and didn't celebrate Christmas. I showed up the last week of the regular season and right on time for the DBs Christmas gift exchange. By now I was used to explaining that Muslims didn't celebrate Christmas, but I wasn't quite prepared for what happened that year. As the DBs finished up the exchange, the boldest, most outspoken man of the group and Texas native, Michael Adams, approached me.

"Wassup, Abdullah?"
"Nothing much, Mike. What's up?"
"Just seein wassup. I know you didn't think you was just gone sit in here all quiet and stuff."
"I'm chilling. I'm good."
"I'm sure you good, but you part of the group now."

"All right."

"So here you go." He reached out to hand me an envelope.

"Nah, I'm cool. I don't celebrate Christmas." I responded while politely putting my hand to my heart.

"I know, but I got you something." He extended the envelope again, this time with a little more authority.

"You didn't have to do that."

"I know, but you family now."

"That's what's up." I smiled with his acknowledgment.

"So I got you a little something. It ain't much. Just a little ole gift card to Best Buy." This time he looked me in my eyes as he tried to maneuver the envelope into my hands.

"I appreciate it but I'm good. I don't..."

"Look, Abdullah. I know you don't celebrate Christmas, but we give gifts in here. We brothas." Mike said as a last gasp attempt.

"I understand." I said letting down my defense.

"So please...take this." He thrust the envelope into my chest.

"All right, Mike." I said conceding the stalemate.

"Yeah, get a little somethin for ya kids or somethin."

"I appreciate this, Mike."

"Umm hmm. Already."

Mike walked away with his head high, chest poked out and feeling a few inches taller. He had just done the unthinkable. He'd given a Christmas gift to a Muslim co-worker.

I hadn't heard someone say "Already" like that since Darrent passed away. It was a Dallas thing. It made me smile thinking about D. Will. I was also smiling because I had been accepted into the group. I was considered family. Now I had to go out and produce on the field, or they'd probably ask for their gift card back.

Our season ended in the second round of the playoffs, where we lost to the eventual Super Bowl champions, the New Orleans Saints. A game that saw many of our starters knocked out of the game—including future Hall of Fame quarterback Kurt Warner.

The Saints were the new "Greatest Show on Turf," with quarterback Drew Brees at the helm. Their running backs and wide receivers were track stars. Their offense was quick hitting, fast-break football. No need for football cleats; we should have brought track spikes. During the first quarter on a routine run play, I noticed our starting safety, Antrel Rolle, walking gingerly towards the sideline.

Uh oh.

We were about to see if all that running I did was helpful.

The baton was passed to me.

"Stick!"

I felt like a minivan with four donuts, jumping into the Daytona 500. They ran circles around me. Three weeks ago I wanted a race to run in, but I never imagined being in the same Heat as the World's Fastest Men. After the game I apologized to some of my teammates and coaches for not being able to keep up. They assured me it was a collective effort and every man in our locker room needed to go home and prepare for the next race.

The next season.

The 2010 season should have been scratched from the record books. Immense turnover at key positions paired with a myriad of injuries equated to a 5-11 record. I didn't escape the injury bug. I missed half the games due to a nagging hamstring injury that hampered me all season. The 2011 season would be a put-up or shut-up season. Put up the numbers or shut up about playing time.

The numbers I needed to match were that of our former special teams captain, Jason Wright. He was a stalwart contributor to the special teams and offensive units. There was no way I could match his offensive output, but I had a chance to contribute on special teams. Not only was he a great player, he was also a great leader. He led film sessions, walkthrough practices, and even led Bible study.

I had my work cut out for me. I began working on my body. I ate natural foods, I worked out using only resistance bands, and I hired a stretching coach. The most important factor in my production equation was me staying on the field. My goals were simple: (1) play all 16 games; (2) lead the team in special teams tackles, and (3) compete for the starting safety job.

The last goal wasn't measurable, but I knew that if I prepared, it would be mine. After developing my body, I worked on my mind.

I watched film of our offense, our opponents' offenses, our defense, and the top defenses in the league. I also studied special teams film ad nauseam.

I memorized the different route combinations, tendencies, and player comforts. It was my first time studying individual players at length. I noticed what the individual players liked to do and what they didn't like. The one consistent thing the offensive players didn't like was: getting hit.

I needed to increase my physicality with opposing players. I didn't need to look far for an example. I watched my big brother Adrian Wilson's individual tape. Adrian *was* the Arizona Cardinals. He was a perennial pro bowler, game-changing defender, and the definition of physical.

As the NFL tried to quiet lawsuits and promote a—phantom—safer game, Adrian became the poster child of what the NFL would no longer tolerate. Big hits, aggressive play, and an intimidating presence. Adrian played with an attitude and an intense desire to make his opponents miserable. This wasn't limited to the players on the field. He wanted to ruin offensive coaches' nights as well. He did that by lining up in unconditional and unpredictable spots. He would say, "If the coaches don't know where you're going to be, they can't account for you."

I began imitating Adrian in practice.

I played with my alignment pre-snap along with my intimidation of the offensive players. Constant bumping, subtle shoves, and trash talking began to unnerve the offensive players and coaches.

It was working.

I just needed to take the same approach into the games. As my defensive play improved, so did my special teams play. I was counted on to lead film sessions, teach new players, and come up with play suggestions.

My on the field contributions were shaping up, but I needed to do more off the field. It wasn't enough for me to do the standard team appearances, so I searched for other opportunities.

The local mosque, Islamic Center of the East Valley, had a number of programs I lent a hand in. I did it not to earn credit, but to show my appreciation. I finally understood what it meant to be a role model and welcomed the responsibility. I began using social media to engage personally with fans as well as mentor younger players. I was starting to find my niche in Arizona.

19

MY TIME

Whether I liked it or not, I was setting an example for people to follow. My teammates, my community members, and my followers on social media. I started doing speaking engagements, hosting fan get-togethers, and leading a youth group. Things were coming together nicely. Then something unexpected happened.

Adrian tore his bicep, and his status for the season was up in the air.

I was his primary backup and presumed replacement until he got healthy. Like Lynch did when I arrived in Denver, Wilson took me under his wing when I arrived in Arizona.

We constantly talked outside of football and developed a strong relationship. He told me not to worry about him but to take the opportunity and run. I hurt for my big brother, but I wanted to show everyone I was ready to fill his shoes. During the first practice without Adrian, we had an intra-squad scrimmage. I made an effort to separate myself from the remaining safeties by my play, and I did. I flew around the field, made spectacular tackles, and broke up a few passes. I wanted to stand out.

My teammates and coaches approached me after practice congratulating me on my play. It had been a long road back, but I was back to playing meaningful football. We were given a few days off as the coaches debriefed about the scrimmage, but more importantly, about the status of our defensive captain. We returned from our break to learn that Adrian would opt not to have a season ending surgery, but he would still miss significant time.

My position coach wanted to talk to me about what this meant moving forward.

"Hamza, thanks for coming."

"Of course, Coach, what's going on?"

"As you know, Dubb won't be able to play for a while."

"Yeah. I heard."

"Well, we needed to bring a few other guys in to get us through the preseason."

"Okay."

"So we need you to bring the guys along and get them up to speed."

"What do you mean?"

"We want you to work with the guys and make sure they know what they're doing."

"All right, I can do that, but what about starting?"

"Right now, we feel it's best..."

"Feel it's best for what?"

"We feel it's best to put a guy in who's already been playing and can..."

"That doesn't make sense. How can you put in a guy that's already been playing?"

"Well, not another safety, we're going to move our third corner..."

"Seriously?"

"Well, we..."

"So you're going to put a cornerback in a safety position, instead of putting a safety at the safety position?"

"We like his range and..."

"I've worked for this. I've dedicated my whole offseason to this. I'm ready."

"I know you're ready, but..."

"But? I just showed in the scrimmage what I can do."

"You played well, there's no denying that, but this is the decision we've come to."

"Man...Alright, Coach...I'm out..."

I wanted to leave.

What about all the times I've heard, "Hard work pays off." The times our coach had stood in front of the team and said, "The best players will play."

The times he said I was a starter and they were lucky to have me as a backup. I no longer had faith in the coaching staff. I wanted to do my job and go home.

With Adrian being hurt, it gave an opportunity for a familiar face to rejoin the group. Matt Ware was re-signed and seamlessly placed back into the room. He'd left the Cardinals after a contract dispute earlier that offseason. He understood my pickle but he cautioned me about running away. He told me frankly, "It ain't what you want."

It wasn't what I wanted.

I wanted to be a starting safety in the NFL. A starting safety for the Arizona Cardinals. A major contributor on a team with an opportunity to be a top tier defense. We just needed everyone to buy in and to play up to our potential. I took the slight as an opportunity to invest more. I invested more time into football and prepared as though I was a starter. The starters began coming to me asking what I would do in certain situations and how to play or attack the offenses.

I broke down the coaches' game-plans and poked holes in it. It got to a point where the coaches would ask me if I saw something on film that was a cause for concern and what my opinion on addressing that concern was. I became an unofficial player-coach.

My job was to play at a high level while instructing and leading others. I was no longer fixated on being a starter. I just wanted to win. We didn't do that. We started the 2011 season one and six, with our defense bringing up the rear in every major statistical category in the league. There was no continuity, leadership, or accountability.

Our special teams was a different story.

We had continuity, leadership, and accountability. I liked to believe that I had a hand in that. I took it seriously like the guys before me. Jason Wright, and before him, Sean Morey and before him, Aaron Francisco, and before him, Hanik Milligan. The Cardinals had a long list of stellar special teams performers. I aimed to add my name to that list.

We were playing fantastic with the addition of uber-talented return man, Patrick Peterson. Peterson was a rookie and the fifth overall selection in the NFL Draft. Easily one of the most talented players I ever saw. He was coming along as a cornerback, but where he made his money early was on special teams.

Special teams was one of the few bright spots on the team, but we weren't pleased with our overall record. We held a team meeting during our bye week where players were allowed to vent their frustrations, and I didn't stay quiet.

"Coach, I have something to say."

I placed my notebook on the ground and stood up in the middle of the auditorium style room.

"I want to ask everyone a question. Why are you playing?"
"Why are you playing football?"
"If you're playing to get your name in the paper, to get a check, or to get girls, you're doing it for the wrong reason."
"You have to play this game for the guy next to you."
"This is a team, and we won't win if everyone's playing for themselves."
"Too many guys are worried about their own stats instead of the only stat that matters."
"The win,"
"I want to win."
"I'm tired of losing."
"We don't do the little things that help us win."
"We don't do those things because we don't appreciate where we are."
"You have to appreciate your position and understand you're privileged to be here."
"What everyone needs is a break."
"We need to get away from here so we'll appreciate how fortunate we are."
"I'm taking a break. I'm leaving the country. I want to go as far away from football as I can."

"I suggest everyone get away and come back ready to win the second half of the season."

We returned from the bye week refreshed. We hit the ground running and played inspired football. The offense, the defense, and the special teams came together as one. We played together and we won together. Personal accolades and titles didn't matter.

I was a leader on the team, a leader in the community, and a leader in the resurgence of the Arizona Cardinals. I asked my teammates to play for the guy next to them and led by example. I led from the rear. I had to play my position in order for our team to succeed. My position was as a mentor and motivator.

I became a man in Denver, a Muslim in Cleveland, and a mentor in Arizona.

20
MONEY TIME

There's an old adage repeated during NFL training sessions and practices: "It's not a sprint, it's a marathon." My career mirrored that of a marathon runner. The best runners know when to coast and when to sprint.

I chose to sprint the last stretch, the final game of the season. I played well all season, leading the special teams unit, as well as being a leader in the locker room. I knew a strong performance would aid me in my offseason contract negotiations. I put forth another solid performance as we snipped the Seattle Seahawks in overtime 23-20. It was our fourth overtime victory of the season and it allowed us to finish the season eight and eight. One game short of making the playoffs. Not bad for a team that started one and six, with a six game losing streak.

After the game, I exchanged jerseys and autographs with my teammates. I'm not sure what preempted me to do this but I'm glad I did. This was the group of men that had assisted me in my race. There were times in my race I wanted to stop running. Times where I didn't understand why I was running or where I was heading. Now I was headed into an uncertain future. I needed clarity from a reliable source. I called my agent CJ Laboy to discuss my future.

"Hello?"
"What's up CJ? This is Hamza."
"Oh what's up, Hamz? I was just talking about you."
"I hope it was good."
"Hamz, it's always good when I talk about you."

73

"That's what I like to hear. CJ, what's the deal with the Cardinals?"

"I was just talking with Rod, the Cardinals General Manager, and they want you back."

"That's good to hear."

"Yeah, I'm supposed to see them at the Combine next week and we'll sit down and talk."

"CJ, I'm tired of playing on one year deals."

"I know you are brother. Your day is coming."

"I just don't want to keep moving Alexa and the children around. I want stability."

"I hear you, Hamz. You know I'm going to go to bat for you."

"They wanted me to step into a role, and I did that."

"You sure did."

"I stayed healthy, I was one of the top producers on Special Teams, and I was a leader on the team."

"They can't deny that, Hamz."

"I want a multiyear deal, CJ."

"You deserve it."

"I know my role here and if I accept this role, I'd like to be fairly compensated for it."

"No doubt, Hamza."

"Top special teams guys around the league average about $1.5 million a year. That's what I want."

"And you deserve every penny, Hamz."

"If AZ doesn't want to do a long term deal, I don't mind going somewhere else, but if I leave, it has to be for an opportunity to start."

"Hamz, I know you're a starter and I know you want to play...we'll get you there."

"I just think this is a big year for me and I have a huge opportunity to do something great."

"I feel it too."

"One more thing, CJ."

"What's that?"

"I've always dreamed of playing on the same team as Husain. If that option is available, I'd like to actively pursue it."

"Of course, Hamza. We have to see what Minnesota wants to do with Husain, but I won't shut any doors."

"Thanks, CJ."

"Anything for you, Hamza."

"All right, I gotta go. I hear one of my little ones doing something they're not supposed to be doing."

"All right, Hamza. Go take care of the fam and I'll take care of the business."
"That's why they pay you the big bucks, CJ."
"Yes, sir."
"Thanks again, CJ."
"Anytime."

I felt better after speaking with my longtime agent. CJ also represented my brother Husain, who was also a free agent after his fourth year with the Vikings. We've been through a lot together, and CJ's always had my best interest at heart. We didn't agree on every decision but I always felt he was a straight shooter.

I know some agents who make unrealistic promises to their clients, but CJ wasn't that type of guy. He was a great caddie for me. He'd instruct me on what he thought would be my best course of action, then he would sit back, await my decision, and watch me swing. I swung and missed a lot during my career but he would always retrieve my club, wipe it clean, and hand me another one. I wasn't sure which club I would need next, but I prepared as if I were going to use each one in my bag.

21
PRACTICE MAKES PERMANENT

In the game of golf, the most important club is the putter. The putter in my bag, is my religion. It may have taken me a while, but I began to put first things first. Although the club that gets the most attention and adulation is the driver, it's not the most important club. The driver in my bag is football. I'm known and celebrated as a football player, but it's not all that I am. The often overlooked clubs in a bag are the irons. The irons are my family. They had been ignored far too often during my career. Now was the time for me to dust them off and improve my relationship with my irons.

I needed to hit the driving range.

I started with my putter. I began going to the mosque—ICEV—for the five daily prayers. After prayer, I read the Qur'an and helped keep the prayer hall clean. This gave me a head-start on the day. After the predawn prayer—Fajr—I raced home to meet my awakening children.

It was time to work on my irons.

Family time was all that mattered to Alexa, Layla, and Aqil. We went to the park, rode bikes, and went swimming. We also did karate and ceramics as a family. I wanted to make up for being an absentee father during the season. Alexa operated as a single mom for much of the year. She never complained, but I found out just how tough it was when she went away for a night on a girls' trip. My pride was the only thing that prevented me from calling her and begging her to come home. I understood the importance of both parents operating as a team. We carved out a schedule that wouldn't place too much weight on either of our shoulders. Our family began to bond. My iron game was coming together well.

After quality time spent on my irons and putter, it was time to bring out the big stick.

My driver.

My driver needed a detailed evaluation if I wanted to continue on the Pro Tour. Safeties are judged on two factors. Tackling and interceptions. My tackling was good, but I needed it to be great. I didn't play on defense so my interceptions were non-existent.

To improve my tackling, I needed to improve my flexibility and lower body strength. To improve my catching ability, I needed to work on my hand strength, hand-eye coordination, and grip.

I enrolled at the Fischer Institute in Tempe, AZ. Brett Fischer was a tenured Physical Therapist for the Arizona Cardinals and operator of his own performance gym. Fischer created a program for me that would satisfy my needs. I was hard at work when I got a call from my younger brother Husain.

March 20, 2012

"*Assalamu Alaikum*, Hamza, what's up?"
"*Wa alaikumu salam*, just finishing up this workout, what's up?"
"Nothing much, just sitting here thinking."
"Thinking about what?"
"Something big..."
"Like what?"
"Hamza, let's go for Hajj."
"When?"
"Now. This year."
"I don't know...I'm still talking to the Cardinals about bringing me back."
"I know, but I think we have to do this, and we have to do it now."
"Well, Hajj is like in October or something right?"
"Yeah."
"You know what this means, right?"
"Yeah."

"We won't be able to sign now; we'd have to wait until we came back."
"Yeah, I'm cool with that."
"I just want you to know it's tough to get signed in the middle of the season."
"Our teams will know and understand."
"I don't know…what if we don't get signed when we come back?"
"*In shaa Allah* we'll deal with that when we get back. Just make *duaa*."
"All right, *in shaa Allah*, I'll ask Allah for guidance and to make it easy for us."
"This is the right thing to do. The time is now. We have money and we're healthy."
"You're right, and I would hate to waste it now, and later wish I would have gone."
"Let's just make *duaa*."
"All right. *In shaa Allah*."

I hung up the phone thinking about my future. Thinking about my offseason goals. Thinking about my clubs. All adult members of the Islamic faith are required to go on the Hajj pilgrimage at least once in their lifetime, if they have the health and wealth to go. This decision wasn't going to be easy. To go for Hajj I would have to table the negotiation talks with the Cardinals.

I figured the decision wouldn't sit well with them if I chose to go.
In the NFL, they want their players to believe football is the only thing that matters. Football was important, but there were other parts of my life that were also important. I sensed it would be tough to return to the NFL, but I was hopeful. Husain decided the time was now to take the Hajj pilgrimage to Mecca.

Husain and I were not bound by any contracts, so we wouldn't be going back on our word or our team. Husain was adamant about fulfilling the fifth pillar of our Islamic faith at that moment, but I wasn't as convinced. I was unsure and I wavered on my final decision to go. I was 28 years old coming off a productive year. I knew it was the time for me to secure some guaranteed money but Husain kept saying, "Now is the time."

I prayed until I too felt it was the right time.

It was Husain's first time as a free agent and he wanted to exercise his absolute freedom by taking his talents to Saudi Arabia. We did most things together, and I didn't want to leave him alone on this decision. I had a feeling this would substantially affect our careers. I prayed for a positive reaction but prepared for a negative one. After much prayer and deliberation, we decided to embark on the journey. I began the offseason working on my putter; now we'll see how I do with it as the only club in my bag.

The Abdullah Brothers, as we became known, were going for Hajj.

22

HAJJ

Breaking News

"**P**omona, CA-Pomona natives, brothers and NFL players Hamza and Husain Abdullah are putting football on the back burner to fulfill the pressing religious obligation of Hajj..."

The response was immediate.

"...To piss out millions of dollars for this crap religion—surely they lost their mind..."
"Great, more terrorists in the making..."
"There is no limit to what religious delusions will drive people to..."
"Frankly, I could give a rat's arse about these two who now have decided to join a cult..."
"Morons..."

Not all the press was bad, but the response to it, outside of the Muslim community, seemed to be. It was ignorance rather than understanding. The individuals who took the time to listen understood where we were coming from and wished us well. The others, who brought their preconceived notions about Islam into the equation, used this as an opportunity to debase our faith. We weren't harming anyone. We were adhering to a tenant of our faith.
This was our faith. I thought about the ramifications of us going to Hajj while listening to a borrowed CD.

"This is My Faith, My Voice!
My Faith, My Voice!
Don't care what they say,
It's my voice.
My Faith, My Voice!"

I looked at the CD Case: Native Deen-*My Faith My Voice*. Native Deen was a group of talented musicians from the East Coast who made quality music with great messages. The message of this song came right on time.

"You will be your faith, I will be mine,
Let's live in peace, *Ma'asalaam*,
Peace all the time, for all mankind, that's on my mind.
My master-plan,
That's my master-plan.
Yeah.
That's my master-plan."

This was our master plan as well. We were making this decision, about our futures, on our own. We're advocates of people being able to live freely and worship as they wish. I didn't understand the detractors. I knew teammates who were Mormon and left football for two years, and people were okay with that. We were going to be gone for two weeks, yet, we were morons. Luckily we didn't do it for them. We did it for us.

We did it with our parents in mind. They taught us to be unapologetically Muslim. To want for our brother what we wanted for ourselves and to stand up for what was right, even if we were standing alone. Thank God we didn't have to be alone on this trip.

My parents and older brother Abbas, would join us.

Abbas made sacrifices in his life that aided us in ours. He was the guinea pig in the Abdullah household who started playing football. We didn't know where football would take us. Now it's taking us to Hajj. With the 2012 NFL season in full swing, we were on a different team flight, headed to a different stadium in a different land.

81

23
WHY ARE YOU HERE?

We arrived safely into The Kingdom of Saudi Arabia wearing new team colors—white.

There is no distinction between rich and poor in appearance during the Hajj pilgrimage. Men wear two plain white cloths called *ihram*. No logos, trademarks, or brand names. It was very different from my football uniform. There were other rules and rituals we needed to learn and understand to make sure we were performing our Hajj correctly. The head coach of our team was Imam Sulaimaan Abdul-Hamed. He and his wife created a group—Hajj Pros—to assist American Muslims in their Hajj.

Imam Sulaimaan was gracious enough to allow us to join his group although we were late in the Hajj process. Many people book their trips a year or at least months in advance. Hajj spanned five days. Five days we would remember for the rest of our lives. What we hoped would be a spiritual journey turned out to be a test of will, patience, faith, and strength. This wasn't the dumbbell or barbell strength, this was true strength. The strength of the mind.

The question arose daily: "Why are you here?"

I began an internal investigation.

"What will you do if the Cardinals don't want you anymore? They were 4-0 when you left, they'll probably end up winning the Super Bowl, too." "How will you handle that?"
"Will you be jealous of your teammates and regret your decision?"

"What will you do when you get back?"

I didn't know. I went back to my golf bag. The putter was there, but so were the driver and irons. I realized I would be incomplete if I only had one club in my bag. I was born in America for a reason. I was Muslim for a reason. I played in the NFL for a reason.

All of these factors were contributing to my overall identity. I was an African-American Muslim NFL Player, who was married with children.

It was okay to be Muslim and be in the NFL.

It was okay to be married and be in the NFL.

It was okay to be in the NFL.

I didn't have to choose the NFL over Islam or vice versa. This is why I am here. To learn. To learn about myself and to learn moving forward: (1) pleasing God does not mean displeasing yourself, (2) all people are created equally but our tests are not and (3) you may get away with lying to people, but you can't lie to yourself.

I'm a football player. That was the truth. I knew it and I loved it. This was the talent I was blessed with. This was my space. This was my calling. I couldn't wait to get back to the states and train for a historic comeback to the NFL.

24
RETURN OF THE MUSLIMS

We were scheduled to return home on October 30, but Hurricane Sandy shut down the entire east coast and prevented us from leaving Saudi Arabia. After a few days of heavy prayer, we were able to go home. The first thing I did when I got home was organize a training schedule. We packed up our Arizona home and moved to Southern California to be closer to my parents and prepare for a return to the gridiron. I enlisted three of the best trainers in the country. A man with an iron grip, a Super Bowl champion, and an Olympic gold medalist; Travelle Gaines, Jason David, and Shawn Crawford.

Travelle would work on my strength, stabilization, and foundation.

Jason worked on my football specific movements and footwork.

Shawn worked on my speed, endurance, and stamina.

We worked out two, sometimes three times a day. I gave myself three weeks to get back into football shape. I circled Monday, November 26 on my calendar. That was the day I would host a workout and return to the NFL. The day came and went. CJ explained, there was no interest from NFL teams. The team I thought would be interested, was Arizona. After a 4-0 start, the team lost five games in a row. They were sure to welcome me back.

I texted CJ and his reply was, "Not Yet."

Despite posting training videos online, phone calls from CJ, myself and Husain, the NFL wanted nothing to do with us. The response was unanimous: "They missed training camp and Organized Team Activities, they're not ready to play football. Maybe next year."

That wasn't the truth.

We were ready. We were healthy. We were anxious.

In 2009, I was signed after sitting at home for 14 weeks. I was out of shape. Now, in 2012, I was faster than I'd ever been, stronger, and wiser. I was a better player. All I wanted was a chance to prove it. I would have to wait until the next season to work out and find an NFL home. The Cardinals finished with a dismal 5-11 record, with most of the decision makers being fired. My best chance at a return took a blow.

I continued the workouts into the offseason and began working out with players soon to be drafted in the 2013 NFL Draft. Before the draft class checked in, I primarily worked out alone or with Husain. I didn't know what type of shape I was in, but I felt great. It wouldn't take long before the whispers started. The incoming rookies asked my trainer about my story.

"Travelle, who is that?"
"That's Hamza Abdullah?"
"Who? Why does he train so hard?"
"He's trying to get back to the NFL?"
"Get back? Where'd he go?"
"He took a sabbatical, and now he's eager to get back."
"Does he ever get tired?"
"He can't afford to get tired and neither can you...you'll learn."

I put everything I had into returning to the NFL. I knew by working hard and doing what I could control, good news was bound to come.

It did.

The Monday after the Baltimore Ravens defeated the San Francisco 49ers in Super Bowl XLVII, Husain would be working out for the Kansas City Chiefs. They were doing a complete overhaul of the team and wanted to start by adding high character guys. This was the first domino. After

Husain killed his workout, they would see he was ready to play, then sign him. After Husain signed, that would let the teams know I was just as committed and ready to get back to playing football.

Husain was signed by the Chiefs and the comeback was halfway complete. My brother stood up for what he believed in, sacrificed his career, led his family to Hajj, and returned to the NFL. It was a storybook ending to an already impressive tale of trial and triumph. I texted CJ asking if he had any good news for me. His response was still, "Not yet."

I wondered when my turn would come. I couldn't worry about it. I needed to continue working out and prepare for the day I did get good news. February turned into March, which creeped into April, without me getting a call.

CJ had the same response whenever we talked. "Not yet."

I wasn't sure how much more my body could take, I could take, or my family could take. Alexa had recently given birth to our third child, Maryam. We were still in LA renting an expensive apartment, paying for workouts, and homeschooling our children.

After six months of constant training without a call, I reached out to one of my ex-teammates who was now in the front office of an NFL team.

"Hello?"
"George, what's up? This is Hamza."
"What's up, bro?"
"Man, just getting done a workout, trying to get some intel."
"Of course, bro...I respect what you and your brother did. That took some guts."
"Thanks, bro. God willing, we're just trying to do what we say and say what we do."
"You've always been like that, bro."
"Man, I appreciate that more than you know."
"Already...but what's good?"
"Man, I'm trying to see what the deal is with my situation. What are people saying?"
"You already know what they're saying."
"Like what?"
"That you're a hell of a player and you can come in and contribute right now."

"But?"

"But, they don't know where you are physically or if you're going to leave again."

"Seriously? I've tried to make it as clear as I could that we only had to do Hajj once."

"You know how these cats are. They don't listen to understand. Whatever the masses think, they think."

"That's sad...What else are they saying?"

"That you could probably come in and compete to start but they don't want to pay you."

"Come on, really?"

"Yeah. They'd rather take a rookie with a minimum salary."

"Even if he's not the player I am?"

"Yep. That's the business, bro. You've been in it long enough to know."

"I have, but I was hoping for at least a workout. I just want to get in front of them so I can show them I'm ready and clear up any misunderstandings."

"Well, we just finished up our offseason roster and started OTAs, so we're not bringing in anyone right now."

"Dang..."

"Don't worry, bro. If anything changes, I'll let you know. Just keep your head up and keep grinding."

"I will. I appreciate the time, George."

"Of course, bro. Give my best to your brother and your family."

"Thanks, George."

"Yes, sir."

The business of football.

I'm well versed in it. I've been a business decision in a few of my previous stops. It didn't derail me but it did make things tougher.

I thought about a way to clarify the misconception that I wasn't committed to the game. I instructed CJ to make it clear to teams that I was starving to prove myself. All I wanted was a chance to work out.

CJ kept singing the same tune. "Not yet." Frustration set in. I was doing everything in my power to get back to the NFL, but it wasn't happening. What's going on? Why aren't they calling? They weren't calling me, so I started calling them. I called the front offices of the Cardinals, Broncos, and New England Patriots. I wasn't looking for a promise or a handout. Just an opportunity to work out.

It was all ignored.

The NFL felt I turned my back on them by going to Hajj, so they turned their back on me. The message was clear. I would no longer be an NFL player. I stopped doing two and three workouts a day. I started focusing my attention on the next chapter of my life.

I booked speaking engagements at Yale, West Virginia, Columbia, Syracuse, Michigan State, Indiana, and NYU. I wrote and submitted 10 treatments proposing television shows I wanted to create. I updated my résumé and applied to coaching positions at USC, the University of La Verne and with the NFLPA's coaching internship. I applied for graduate school at Southern Methodist University in Dallas, TX. I wrote a children's book, with the hopes of having a series published. I created a Physical Education program for a private school. I started a Boot Camp. I filed the paperwork and built a website for a marketing and management group that my family wanted to start. I drew up plans for a sports complex, performance gym, and grocery store. I began preliminary work on an audiobook I wanted to create, titled *10 Minute Pro Bowler*. I discussed investment opportunities with entrepreneurs and began vetting every proposal. I was busy.

I was taking action. I wasn't going to sit around and be sad. I wanted to handle my business. I also wanted to see what help the NFL and NFLPA gave to former players. I was told not to call them until I was 100% certain I wasn't returning to the field of play.

No problem. I was sure they would be there when I needed them.

I was sadly mistaken.

25

WAKE UP

"I'm done."

I knew it. Every athlete knows. We pretend, we smile for the camera, we tell outsiders not to doubt us, but our mind is made up.

We're done.

When the passion to prepare no longer matches the passion to compete, it's over. I had been preparing with no competition in sight. I couldn't see the finish line because I had already passed it.

While I was playing I made a checklist of goals I wanted to accomplish when I retired: (1) own a home, (2) own cars for my wife and me, (3) and have enough money to live two years without employment. I was blessed to check every box. I'm not sure what preempted me to save enough money for two years, but I'm glad I did.

I didn't foresee a scenario that kept me unemployed for two years but I planned nonetheless. School was my first option. I wanted to learn a better way to organize, facilitate, and execute a program to assist in the transition of student-athletes.

My senior year in college, I was one of four players on the football team to make it to the NFL. Nineteen members from that team would eventually make it to the NFL. Our roster consisted of 115 players. That meant 96 players would never play football again. We may say, "Who cares, now they get to enter the real world," but football *was* their real world. They've put in the same amount of time, sacrifice, and injuries, as the guys who made it to the NFL.

They've also been playing since they were kids.

I started late at the age of 12. I graduated college at 21. That's nine years of football for a late bloomer. A majority of my friends and teammates started when they were seven years old. Some as early as five. Then in an instant, it's gone.

"Well, if they were smart, they'll have their degree to fall back on."

At least that's what we tell ourselves. Yet our days, weeks, and semesters revolve around our seasons. We're herded into undemanding majors to ensure our time away from the field is spent studying playbooks, not course books. We're not student-athletes, we're athlete-students. Being an athlete at a four year college or university is a full-time job that prepares us to be professionals in the sport we play.

What about the 98% of senior NCAA football players who don't go pro?

I want to address that.

Back in 2009, I proposed a liaison position between the athletes, the coaches and the administrators to my alma mater. The position I proposed would include all athletes and would not be controlled by the head football or head basketball coach. It would be impossible to have the athletes' best interest at heart, when their head coach is my boss. I began studying and reading about transition, the way of transition, and how to properly transition from life's roadblocks. I didn't take the position because I ended up going back to play. Now that I am done playing, I realized that to properly aid in the transition of other athletes, I myself needed to transition.

"What would I be transitioning to?"

I've been known as a football player for nearly 20 years. What would I be now? I became known as a public speaker and even updated my LinkedIn profile to accentuate the change. Even during my appearances, the question kept coming up: "What are you doing now?"

Speaking wasn't enough.

The audience wanted to know what I was doing, not what I was saying.

I needed a title.

The television treatments I submitted weren't responded to. The coaching applications got lost in the mail—although I sent them by way of email. The children's book and audiobook needed work before being published. The PE program was a go, as long as I didn't expect payment. The graduate school said yes if I could make it to Dallas in a few weeks. The marketing and management group is still a few years off as is the sports complex, performance gym, and grocery store. The investment opportunities didn't comply with what I was looking for in a company to grow with.

I put too much into the Boot Camps. I created a schedule and detailed regimen—like the ones we have in the NFL—but participants were just happy to be doing pushups with a professional athlete. It was much tougher than I anticipated to get going in the right direction.

I can't go back to the NFL.

I have no choice but to finally Transition. I accomplished my childhood dream of playing in the NFL, but just like any other dream, eventually I had to wake up.

26
I KNOW EXACTLY WHAT TO DO

I woke up in a strange new world. A world where the demand and motivation to get better wasn't evident. I took the same approach I took in football with my proposed projects. I would grind and grind until the product was finished. Until the proposal met the requirements for submission. In football, we receive instant criticism and are able to correct the mistakes and show a full understanding of what's required. It didn't work like that during the transition.

There was no response.

I was my own player, coach, and team. There was no true measure as to whether or not I had gotten better. I reached out to CJ and the NFLPA to see if they could assist me with my projects. I wanted a mentor to talk me through the steps of transition but also to point me in the right direction of individuals who could offer professional evaluations of my proposals. CJ was my man. I depended on him to give me clarity throughout my career. It was only natural that I reached out to him when I felt stuck in the mud. CJ didn't know how to respond. I was his first client to ask about post-NFL business.

He directed me to the NFLPA.
To CJ's defense, an agent's priority is to maximize their clients worth while they're in the league. It's not to hold our hand after we retire. After serving two years as a player representative for the NFLPA, I had an intimate knowledge of the individuals working there and the benefits for retired players. I was 100% sure I wasn't going back to play, so I phoned the organization that would assist in my transition. After all, that's what I was told to do when I was an active player.

"Benefits."

"Hi, my name is Hamza Abdullah, a recently retired seven year veteran. I was calling for a little help."

"What kind of help?"

"What...ever...kind...of...help...you're...offering."

"Well, do you want benefits, 401(k), tuition reimbursement...?"

"Honestly, I just retired and I don't know where to start."

"Okay, let me see, what was your last name again?"

"Abdullah. A, B as in Boy, D as in Dog, U, L, L, A, H as in Henry."

"Hamza?"

"Yes, ma'am."

"Okay, so the last date you were on a team was...March 12, 2012?"

"Yes, ma'am."

"Okay, so the first thing, is your severance."

"Yes, ma'am, I've already received that."

"Okay, so now what do you need?"

"I know about the tuition reimbursement plan, but what else do you have for retired players?"

"Well, I can send you our retirement playbook and you can see what's in there."

"The purple one?"

"Yeah."

"Well, I have one of those already, but it's not really much help."

"Well, it details your benefits."

"I read the entire book but it wasn't clear what to do first or the process."

"Well, I can send you an application and you can apply for the benefits."

"Do I need to do anything else?"

"No, just apply, and you'll be taken care of after that."

"Okay...and I want to go back to school, how does the tuition reimbursement plan work?"

"Well, as it says, we don't pay for it, you do. And you have to keep a certain GPA and keep all of your receipts, then the following year you'll be reimbursed."

"Okay, does it matter where I go to school or how much it costs?"

"It doesn't matter the college, university, or learning institute as long as it's accredited and you have receipts."

"Okay, and the cost?"

"We'll match up to $40,000."

"Wow, that's cool."

"Yes, and you have five years to file for this."

"Okay...I have another question."
"Yes?"
"I'm looking for someone who can help me with a few proposals or someone who can help me in my transition. Is there anyone that could help me with that?"
"I'll see if I can put you in contact with someone that can help you."
"Okay, thank you."
"Is there anything else?"
"No. Thank you."
"Thank you for calling."

The call was informative and beneficial. I learned exactly how the tuition reimbursement worked along with receiving applications to file for my other benefits. I anticipated the call back from a mentor to point me in the right direction. I learned that the various pension plans and accounts I'd heard about when I was playing were indeed retirement plans; plans that did not issue money when I actually retired, but when I reached retirement age. As Deniece would say, "Silly me."

When I received the application for benefits, I asked my wife to fill them out, then sent them back. The benefit I felt I qualified for was the Line of Duty Disability Benefit, or LOD. The LOD is in place to help during an NFL Players transition. The player has to show a substantial percentage of total body disability to qualify for the seven year benefit.

As I learned information on retirement and transition, I forwarded that information to other players. Many players were shocked to hear of the LOD benefit. It would help my family and other player families out there. I wondered why this wasn't widely known in NFL player circles. I guarantee players would have a smoother transition if they knew of all the benefits available to them. This benefit may seem small, but it can have a huge impact.

I was in the process of getting my finances in order. There was no more football, thus no more training. I moved my family from our apartment in LA to a townhouse in Diamond Bar, CA. It reduced our expenses while still allowing us to stay close to my parents.

We decided to stay in Southern California due in large part to Abu Shante's deteriorating health. Due to a work injury, the once brawny man was now walking with a cane, on top of being dialyzed every other day. I thought about moving back up to our house in Seattle, but my parents would have been demoralized. My dad liked to sit with my children and watch cowboy movies, and eat snacks I wouldn't approve of. My children's weekend hangout spot was with my parents, and I didn't want to change that.

As my house sat empty, Alexa and I made the decision to sell it. It didn't make financial sense to continue paying for two residences, which could have been three if I went back to school or was hired for a coaching position. I had the itch to coach, but the opportunity wasn't right. I took it upon myself to go back through my old notebooks filled with plays, tendencies and scouting reports.

I diagnosed film and broke down teams as if I were coaching. I attended local high school football games—to the astonishment of the parents in the stands—I called out the plays before they happened. I knew coaching was what I wanted to do. I'd follow in Coach Yusuf's footsteps.

Coach Abdullah had a nice ring to it.

27
COACH ABDULLAH

My first call as Coach Abdullah went to my former special teams coach, Kevin Spencer. He was fired by the Cardinals after the 2012 season and landed in San Diego, with the Chargers. I always dreamt of playing close to home, but coaching would be even better.

"Hello."
"Hey Coach Spence, what's up? This is Hamza Abdullah."
"Well I'll be darned. Hamza, how are you?"
"I'm doing well Coach, just trying to transition from the game."
"Don't transition too far from the game."
"It's funny you mention that Coach, that's what I wanted to talk to you about."
"Oh yeah?"
"Yeah, Coach. I wanted to see if you guys had any openings or opportunities where I could come down and get into coaching."
"Hamza, you're going to make a great coach. I've always told you that."
"Thanks, Coach."
"Now, we're just wrapping up our offseason program and preparing for training camp."
"Okay."
"I think we're set for now at the coaching spots, but I'll see what I can do."
"Thanks, Coach."
"Anything for you, Hamza."
"Coach, I really appreciate you taking the time to talk with me, and I really appreciated my time in Arizona playing for you."
"Hamza, you're a special player and one of my favorites."

"Thank you, Coach."

"No, thank you. You were a pleasure to coach and you made my job much easier."

"I thank you for standing up for me and allowing me to play."

"It was a no brainer. You were one of our best players."

"Thank you, Coach."

"Anytime...Look, I'll talk to Whiz and see what we can do."

"Again, I truly appreciate it...this is my cell phone number, so you can just reach me here."

"Sounds good, Hamza. Thanks for calling."

"Thanks again, Coach. Talk to you soon."

"Okay. Bye-bye."

"Peace."

I imagined myself standing on the sideline at Qualcomm stadium on a beautiful San Diego Sunday. The skies were blue without a hint of precipitation in the air. The Blue Angels were flying overhead. I had on my patented—Charger colored—kufi, coaching headset, glasses, and team issued polo shirt tucked into my khaki pants. We were set to kick off against my former team, the Denver Broncos. A division rival and team I desperately wanted to beat. Two evenly matched teams vying for the division crown. Special teams would be the difference in our team prevailing or failing. I wasn't nervous, but I was anxious. I had prepared well and gave the team a fiery speech before the game. They were ready, we were ready, and I was ready...

Waiting for a phone call that never comes is akin to watching the chimney on Christmas Eve.

Santa's not coming because Santa doesn't exist.

The opportunity for me to be a Chargers coach didn't exist. The opportunity for me to go directly from the playing field to the coaching office didn't exist.

I didn't blame Coach Spencer. Coaches are busy people. I understand that. It wasn't his fault. It was the NFL's fault. This is their system. The players play and the coaches coach. The players are not coaches and the coaches are not players.

I began to wonder...

"Wouldn't it make sense to learn a specific technique and skill from someone who has done it before?"

The person who taught me how to drive, was my teammate at Washington State, Virgil Williams. He was a skilled driver, with a car and his driver's license. Why did I choose Virgil? Was it because he's observed driving for the last six years or was it because he was actually driving for six years? I think back to the NFL coach that made the biggest impression on me. It was my first position coach in the NFL, Mike Tomlin. He didn't play in the NFL, but he played football in College. He played wide receiver at the College of William & Mary.

He played the game.

When he coached me, it was believable. I knew he wasn't asking me to do anything he hadn't done before. One of the reasons players throughout my career have listened to my advice is because I've done it. I was one of them. I was a player.
In the NFL: Players play and coaches coach. Who are the coaches? They should be former players.

When Doctors or Lawyers become tenured and proficient in their fields, they are elected to executive boards and become professors at institutions of higher learning.

After NFL players retire from the field of play, the natural transition, should be to coaching or analyzing at the highest level. We are instead relegated to menial positions so that we can learn to "humble ourselves," and to quit being "uppity." The banishment to the football abyss—lower division college football or bad high school football—is done, in the hopes that we quit. We are encouraged to quit by the actions of our perceived superiors to prove the theory that NFL players think they're too good to have a boss or start from the bottom.

This theory is believed in coaching's inner circle, although 54.4% of NFL players were born in a county with a poverty level higher than the national average (Burkmont, 2015).

We originated from the bottom.

NFL players began their lives underprivileged and without adequate resources; yet, they were still able to defy the odds. By attending college and ultimately playing in the NFL, they've shown their work ethic, patience, perseverance, dedication, and determination. All qualities and traits a coach should instill in their players. As a player, it's easier to listen to a coach who's asking you to do something, knowing they themselves have done it. The NFL doesn't believe this logic, and it shows in their hiring practice.

In the NFL, 68% of the Head Coaches, did not play in the NFL.

There are great head coaches that didn't play in the NFL; but why aren't more retired players getting an opportunity to show they can also be great? The head coach must be a great leader of men. He must be able to motivate, inspire, and get the team to coagulate at the right time. He must have a keen knowledge of the game, handle pressure, and manage others. Many retired players showed they can do this during their playing days.

The coordinators are in charge of putting the players in the right situations, which usually constitutes the actual play calling. The offensive and defensive coordinators on the staff aren't former players, either, as only 25% of them played in the NFL. Coordinators are also the next in line to becoming head coaches. If players are not able to become coordinators, how will they become head coaches?

The assistant coaches or position coaches are the keys to the development and success of the individual player, which will constitute the development and success of the entire team. Despite the daily duty of teaching techniques, only 30% of assistant coaches have played in the NFL.

Position coaches should be former players.

I want to know how to do a specific technique from someone who has done it before. I wouldn't let someone who's watched YouTube videos on heart surgeries perform a coronary artery bypass graft on me.

No.

I don't care how long he's watched them. He doesn't know, he thinks he knows. He's never done it. I'd want the cardio thoracic surgeon who has performed 100 successful surgeries and learned from the best heart surgeon in the world to perform the CABG.

It is a matter of life and death.

In the NFL, tackling is a matter of life and death. If I can't tackle, I won't be in the NFL very long, causing the death of my career. I want to learn how to tackle Adrian Peterson from a guy who tackled Eric Dickerson and Tony Dorsett. Not someone who's played Madden their whole life. I'm not saying every player can be a great coach, but every player has the ability and the knowledge to coach.

Every coach can't play.

The general managers are not former players, either. Just 25% of GMs have played in the NFL. These are the individuals in charge of creating the team and evaluating talent. Players have to evaluate talent in seconds while on the field.

When Heisman trophy winner Ron Dayne bursts through the offensive line and down the sideline, I have less than two seconds to evaluate his speed, velocity, ability to change directions, place on his body most susceptible to stopping him, which hand he's carrying the ball in and if he can switch it, where his free hand is, and the probability he uses it to stiff-arm me. If I am able to do this in a matter of seconds, what can I do with hours, days, weeks, or months?

I have played the game of football since 1995. I've studied football at the highest levels since the year 2000. I am well versed in football. It can be argued that not only do I have a Masters, I have a Doctorate in football. I'm a late bloomer that didn't play that much or that long. How is it that I played 12 years of combined collegiate and professional football, but I'm not qualified to coach?

The NFLPA coaching internship responded to my inquiry and informed me I couldn't choose my placement school, and it would most likely be a Division II school; a school lacking an athletic budget, an adequate staff, and any realistic expectations to compete at a higher level. I wanted to compete at the highest level. I wanted to coach at the highest level. The highest level is an NFL head coach. I looked at the plausible way to one day becoming an NFL head coach.

The best way to becoming an NFL head coach is to be a coordinator on a good team, preferably an offensive coordinator. (20 of 32)

The next best thing is to have already been an NFL head coach. (10 of 32)

After the trading of head coaches, the best NCAA Head Coaches get a look. (2 of 32)

That's it.

If you do not fit the above criteria, you won't be a head coach in the NFL. To be an NFL Head Coach, I had to be a coordinator. How does one become a coordinator? Offensive coordinator in particular? I needed to be a quarterbacks coach or assistant head coach. Before being a quarterbacks coach or assistant head coach, I needed to be a position coach. Before I was a position coach, I needed to be a quality control coach. Before that, an intern. How do I become an intern? The head coach has to want me on his staff, meaning he has to know me. I have to be one of his buddies. To be a head coach in the NFL, I needed to be the buddy of an NFL head coach.

NFL head coaches don't have former players as buddies.

We need a better system.

A system that allows the proper transition for qualified candidates—who are passionate about moving forward in the game of football—by providing them with an opportunity at uplifting and transferring key knowledge to other professionals.

Why are we prevented from our natural transition?

The system of transition in the NFL is flawed. The reason players are lost in transition is because they have a glass ceiling above them. They can no longer progress. They can no longer advance their studies or distribute the knowledge they've acquired during their playing career. I believe there are some organizations and head coaches that are getting it right. It's about time the rest of the NFL follow their lead. Coach Abdullah will have to wait for another opportunity; but I'm not discouraged. I'm sure it will happen. *In shaa Allah.*

In the meantime, all I have is time.

28

MAKING THE GAME SAFER

In the name of "Making the Game Safer," the NFL has gone to great lengths to show the public they're doing their part. They've cut practice time, days allocated to training time at the facility, and time with coaches, generally giving players more time off. On the outside, it looks like they're minimizing time to minimize players' exposure to injury, specifically limiting hits to the head. In actuality, it's covering up the insufficiencies in the coaching staff. With less time with the players, the coaches cut out the teaching portion of coaching and emphasize the implementation of the playbook.

Now, the coaches are not exposed to showing their players they don't know the techniques to adequately complete the task. Because the proper techniques are not emphasized, it relates to sloppy play. This sloppy play is then analyzed by individuals who also have not played in the NFL, thus resulting in the stark critique of a player that will result in the shortening of his career. The player was not instructed on the proper technique to begin his career, and his play mirrored that of a man thrown in the deep end of the pool who has never been taught to swim.

He's just trying to save his life.

The swim coach throws the player in the pool, watches from the sideline as the player almost drowns, but miraculously the player makes his way to the edge of the pool. When the players hand finally reaches up and grabs the platform, the coach nods his head as if he is the reason this player didn't drown. The coach is patted on the back and anointed as a "great coach." He'll place the nearly deceased player on his résumé and bio as a player he "oversaw" or "helped."

It's all a farce.

There is no way to make the game safer.

It's football.
Football is a violent sport, and it will forever be a violent sport. The goal of the game is to score on your opponent while inflicting physical, emotional, and psychological damage. In most cases, that damage is irreparable.

I enjoyed it.

Every player enjoyed it. It's the test of a man's will. There was no greater feeling than lining up across from a guy and he's scared to look you in your eyes. He's intimidated by you, and you haven't said a word or laid your hands on him. He'll bow out gracefully soon with a fictitious injury and you'll have done your job.

The gameplay cannot be made safer.

The proper diagnosing of injuries, being honest with a player about his medical history, and treating those injuries is how to make the game safer. Guaranteed contracts for the players is how to make the game safer. Employing qualified personnel to teach proper techniques is how to make the game safer. Health insurance for life after the player leaves the NFL is how to make the game safer.

If there are no players, there will be no game.

I love the game of football, and I don't want it to go away. I'm afraid it will if we don't look at what's happening to the game. It's evolving into an individual sport.

Players are now graded by a group of analytical advisors, who again, have never played the sport and don't understand the intricacies nor the plays. The player is then shown this grade at the end of the season during contract negotiations.

Football is the ultimate team sport. It has always been a team sport, and yes, individual success does lead to team success; but it has to be a group of individuals working as one to achieve that team success.

For example: A normal defensive line has four players. Two defensive ends on the outside and two defensive tackles on the inside. To keep it simple, we'll call this front Even.

In this Even front, we'll have the two defensive ends align head up on the offensive tackles, and the defensive tackles align head up on the offensive guards. The defensive ends are in a "5 technique," while the defensive tackles are in a "2 technique." There are five men on the offensive line, so the Center is the only one who is uncovered. He is the center of the formation and will hike the ball to the quarterback behind him. In this Even front—without any stunts, games or tricks—the defensive line is taught to push forward while staying in their lanes.

Their job is to collapse the pocket of the quarterback and suffocate him. With all the defenders working together, an ideal result is the quarterback releases the ball before he's ready. The idea of this front is not to get a sack, which is what most analytic advisors will grade these players on. Their job is to collapse the pocket. Now, if there is one player in that Even front that decides he wants to get a sack, he will do so at the expense of the integrity of the defense.

If the defensive end on the left side decides he's going to pretend like he's rushing upfield, then does a spin move to the inside in hopes of surprising the offensive tackle—thus getting a sack—he will be sadly mistaken. Not only will he have gotten out of his lane, he will have lost the outside brick of the wall and possibly knocked off the defensive tackle on the left side. Now the entire left side of the defensive line has been breached, and the quarterback will calmly roll to his right and throw a perfect pass; not just for a first down, but possibly a touchdown.

When individuals think it is all about them or they are worried about their individual grade, it is to the detriment of the entire team. There's a place for analytics in football, but it's not on the field of play.

I talk to retired players, and many of them harbor some resentment to the league. They see the "me" guys are the ones who get the big contracts, notoriety, and longevity in the NFL. Most of these retired players were "we" guys; their unselfishness was seen as a point of weakness or unproductiveness. These players were adhering to the rules of the playbook or team. All of this leads them to have an unhealthy view of themselves and the game of football. I felt that I couldn't afford to have an unfavorable view of the game because my brother was still in it.

I watched every Chiefs game, and I wanted him to succeed. I wanted him to prove Muslim football players can go to Hajj and come back to the game of football. I wanted him to do all the things I wasn't able to do during my career. I lived vicariously through him.
Husain was my beacon of light and my lifeline to the locker room. I missed the lifestyle, I missed the camaraderie, I missed the game. Although Husain kept me abreast of the locker room details, I still went through football withdrawals. Honestly, I still do.

When I'm suffering, the first thing I do is pop in my old game tapes. It makes me smile to see me in uniform and making plays. I critique myself and notice where I could have went left instead of right. I review my game, imagining what it would feel like to be back in the meeting room with all of my teammates, laughing at a blunder by our position coach or the sleeping of our star player.

On one of the days I was particularly feeling it, I picked up the phone and called my college roommate and recently retired nine year NFL veteran, Erik Coleman.

"What's up, H?"
"Man, nothing. Just chilling watching old game tapes."
"Haha, you know I be doing that too?"
"For real?"
"Yep."
"Yeah, I miss playing."
"Me too, bro."
"So what do you do now?"
"Everything and nothing."
"Haha, what do you mean by that?"
"I mean, I do everything to try and keep my mind off football, but I do nothing that actually replicates that feeling of playing football."
"That's real right there."
"I know. It's like, what are we supposed to do?"
"I don't know. I thought about coaching."

"I have too, but shoot, I'm only 30. In the NBA, I'd be in my prime. I don't want to stop my career in my prime to coach."

"That's real there. I never thought about it like that."

"Yeah, my last year in Detroit sucked. My DB coach didn't know ~~shit~~ and I was basically coaching everyone."

"I've had that feeling too. My last year in AZ was like that."

"Yeah, and I'm coaching these fools to take my job. So then when they get the gist of it, they cut me."

"That's that stuff I don't like."

"It's a cold game man. They use us because we're professionals, then throw us out."

"And what are we supposed to do after that?"

"They don't care. As long as we shut the ~~fuck~~ up and don't tell everyone how ~~fucked~~ up the league is."

"Man, you're preaching right now."

"It's real. And the ~~fucking~~ NFLPA ain't doing a damn thing about it."

"Man, I called them the other day."

"Did they even answer?"

"Yeah, I asked them for help and they gave me some numbers and sent some forms."

"I bet that's all they gon' do. They don't really be trying to help. That's a shame."

"Man for real. EC, how have you been with your emotions? I feel like sometimes I can't control them."

"It's crazy you said that. The other day I caught myself yelling at my daughter and I didn't even know why I was yelling."

"That's crazy, the same thing happened to me."

"It's serious, bro. I'll go workout and come home and just yell at my wife for no reason."

"There has to be a reason all of this is happening."

"There probably is bro, I don't know."

"I don't either...Well, keep in touch bro, and let me know if you need anything."

"All right H, tell Alexa and the kids we said hi."

"All right, you do the same for your family."

"All right. I love you, bro."

"I love you too, E. Thanks, bro."

Erik has always been a guy I could lean on. He was my roommate in college and the starting safety on our team. He was my big brother, mentor, and example. He helped me get my agent, financial advisor, and personal trainer. He was a player that always played with a chip on his shoulder. He was short in stature but was as competitive as any *big* safety. He stood five foot ten on a good day. If he were my size, he would have been a first round draft pick and recognized as one of the top safeties in the NFL.

Instead, he was often unfairly criticized and ostracized from NFL teams. Despite the exclusion from teams' future plans, he was still able to have a remarkable career. Erik was also a guy who I have and would again take into a fight with me. He was a tough customer, and it was always better to be on his side than across from it. As tough as his shell was, his heart was soft and squishy. He's a sucker for love and he loves his girls. He loves his wife, his mom, and his daughters. I couldn't imagine him raising his voice at any of them.

I have been in his presence when his daughter pulled a freshly made plate of homemade spaghetti onto the floor, and he didn't make a peep. Instead he ran over to make sure she was okay.

Holding her, kissing her, and apologizing to her for him not being more aware of the situation. Erik was a gentle man. If we're both feeling like this, I wonder who else feels like this.

My quest for answers began.

29

POST-CAREER PLAYBOOK

My question was the same when I texted the retired players in my phone book.

"I know you're good, but how do you feel?"

I felt like killing myself...
Like ~~shit~~...
Like, this can't be life...
I don't know. I'm scared though...
Like I need to do something or else...
Mad all the time...
I hate football...

There had to be something to this. Every player, regardless of the tenure in the league, size of the contract, or if that person was currently employed, felt the same way.

When I asked two follow up questions, it was more of the same.

"What do you need? What needs to be done?"

Help...
Football...
Guidance...
Money...
Mentor...
Information. The only information I get, is from you...

Playbook for when we get done...

We needed a playbook for the NFL afterlife. I wanted to create a position for college students transitioning but I didn't think NFL players would have the same need. Financially they should be okay. They should also have enough connections where they can get into another career fairly quickly. Then I thought about my own transition. I needed guidance as well. To attain guidance, one must seek guidance. That's what I set out to do. I started with myself.

I booked a consultation with a psychologist to see if they could help me understand what was going on.

"Good afternoon, Hamza, how are you?"

"I'm doing well."

"Good. You look well."

"Thank you."

"So what brings you in today?"

"I don't know, just trying to see what's going on."

"What's going on?"

"Yeah, I'm starting to feel a little more emotional."

"When do you feel emotional?"

"Lately? All the time it seems."

"Are there any events that trigger it?"

"I'm not really sure...I was watching football the other day..."

"And..."

"And I got mad at some of the players..."

"What do you mean?"

"Well, I was at my trainer's house watching the game, and got mad at some players."

"What happened?"

"One of the players didn't react right away to a play and cost his team a touchdown."

"So what did you do?"

"I grabbed the remote and explained to everyone what the player's job was..."

"You grabbed the remote?"

"Yeah. I stopped the game, rewound it, and explained the play to everyone."

"How did that make you feel?"

"Worthless."

"Why worthless?"

"Because they didn't care. I was the only one that cared, and I was wasting my time."

"Do you feel like you're wasting your time now?"

"No."

"What other times have you felt like you were wasting your time?"

"Well, all the time."

"All the time?"

"Yeah."

"Give me an example."

"Well, like when I take my children to school."

"You feel like you're wasting your time?"

"Yes, because I take them to school, they stay there all day, then when I pick them up..."

"When you pick them up, what?"

"When I pick them up and ask how their day was and what they learned, they say the same thing."

"And what's that?"

"Nothing!"

"And that upsets you?"

"Yes, it upsets me."

"Why does it upset you?"

"Because I'm not doing anything, my children aren't doing anything, it's a life of nothing."

"And what will make you have a life of something?"

"I don't know, but this isn't it."

"I want you to think of something you have coming up. A date, an event, something to look forward to."

"Well, I'm getting inducted into my high school hall of fame."

"See, that's a big deal. That's a something. Congratulations."

"Thank you."

"Do you think they put people who do nothing in the hall of fame?"

"No, they don't."

"What else? Any other upcoming events?"

"Well, I'm going to watch my brother play in the NFL for the first time."

"Isn't that exciting? That's something."

"Yes, it is...it's just weird."

"Why is it weird?"

"Because I know I could be playing too, but I'm not."

"That's understandable. But you are there to support your brother."

"Yes, I am. I just don't want to be jealous or envious."

"Have you been jealous of him?"

"I want to say no, but I don't know. I always try to offer advice and pray for him."

"Well, that's what good big brothers do."

"I know, but it's different now. This is the first time he's playing and I'm not."

"Well, you'll have to remember why you're there. You're there for a reason."

"I know."

"And what reason is that?"

"To support my brother."

"He would do it for you, wouldn't he?"

"He has done it for me."

"Exactly. Hamza, I see a lot of something in your life. Do you?"

"Yes, I do."

"Remember, if you ever find yourself getting upset, think about why you're upset and how you got there."

"Okay I will. Thank you, Doc."

"Thanks for coming."

The walls weren't closing in on me. I did have good things going for me in my life. I just needed to expand my vision. It was tough to see it while I was looking at what others had and I didn't. I needed to continue my therapy sessions, but I also needed to keep in touch with the other players and continue doing research. I'm fortunate to have someone to talk to, but how many other guys aren't so lucky?

30
CTE

On my flight to Kansas City to watch Husain's game, I bought the *League of Denial*. An exposé of the NFL's attempts to hide the long term effects of head trauma in NFL players. The book was written by two investigative reporters for ESPN. Steve Fainaru and Mark Fainaru-Wada came together to unsheathe the NFL's dirty little secret.

Chronic Traumatic Encephalopathy or CTE.

CTE is a degenerative brain condition linked to repetitive hits to the head. The book detailed retired players' struggles with their finances, family life, and emotions after leaving the game. These players were struggling and begging for help, but the NFL turned its back on them. Upon further review, these players suffered from CTE.

The NFL is buying time because as of today, CTE can only be diagnosed posthumously. Time is ticking. Eventually that bomb will go off, and the NFL won't be able to hide.

"How many former players have to kill themselves before you guys ~~fucking~~ realize, that they're pushing us to it?"

Zero. The answer *should* be zero. Instead we get the standard unceremonious statement from the NFL when a player dies by suicide:

"He was a member of our family for _____ years. He still had a lifetime in front of him. Right now all of our thoughts and prayers are with his family during this most difficult time. Thank you for all of your support and consideration."

And that's that.

They'll continue to deflect with disingenuous replies to those inquiring for a better understanding.

This is the way of the NFL. Deny, deny, deny, and when that doesn't work, deny again. I'm done with the denial. I need to know what's going on and try to help. That's going to take more research, acquiring more knowledge and applying that knowledge. I recently read about a former Major League Baseball Player who suffered from CTE at the time of his death. Like most individuals with CTE, he committed suicide.

Suicide.

I've read the CTE signs and symptoms, and I know I exhibit a few of them. Alexa would be the first to tell you I've experienced varying degrees of anxiety, depression, mood swings, and impulsive behavior during my NFL career. I'm not saying I definitely have it, nor do I want to check and see. I don't want to know because if I know I have CTE, I may think like all the other individuals who had it. That taking my own life was the only way to make it better. I believe it will get better. I believe when I get into my routine where I can work every day and travel as I may, that I will be okay. While traveling to KC, I can't help but think about what occurred here less than a year ago.

On Saturday, December 1, 2012, the Kansas City Chiefs were preparing for their match against the Carolina Panthers. The Chiefs players awoke to the shocking news that one of their teammates, Jovan Belcher, had murdered his girlfriend Kasandra Perkins, drove to the practice facility, then turned the gun on himself.

Jovan Belcher would later be found to have CTE.

What a tragedy. An unspeakable tragedy. What was the NFL's response?

"The games must go on."

An active player commits murder then kills himself at the training facility, in front of the heads of the organization, and the NFL's response was to play on.

The level of distaste and dehumanizing of the players was never as apparent as it was at that moment. My heart immediately went to the families, the orphaned daughter, and the Chiefs players. I couldn't imagine playing in a football game after such a tragic event. I pray the families and players were able to seek professional help after an unimaginable tragedy. I ask myself, how can I help? How can I be a part of the solution?

Starting a non-profit organization for athletes, with an emphasis on transitioning athletes, can help. I'll call it Athletes Best Source. Empowering the athletes on and off the field will be the goal. Maintaining our identity as contributing members of society, I believe, can aid in the overall health of transitioning athletes.

I don't want anyone after me to feel the way I do. I don't want any other athlete to think that the only solace will come from holding a gun to his or her head or chest.

I have to be here to protect Alexa. To protect my daughters. To protect my son. I can't let anyone harm my children. I love them too much. My family needs me and I need my family. I have to stand up for them, which in turn, will be me standing up for myself.

31
FIT TO PLAY FOOTBALL

The weekend in Kansas City was a roller coaster of emotions. I was excited to be around the game again but irritated I was doing it next to a guy drinking beer and telling me the other players sucked. I was once one of those other players. I tuned the crowd out and focused on Husain. I wanted to watch him as a proud older brother instead of a coach critiquing his every move. It was enjoyable to watch as the Chiefs beat the Browns, pushing their record to 8-0. Husain was on a winning team and most likely a playoff team. I was excited for his future but unsure of mine.

While in the Midwest, I scheduled a doctor's appointment with a well-known orthopedist in Chicago. I wanted a comprehensive physical exam to see what kind of beating my body took while playing football. On the way to Chicago I sat next to a kind woman who kept looking over at my book. She would periodically ask me questions pertaining to the book then look away for a few minutes, then repeat the cycle. She was fascinated by the football helmet on the cover.

As our plane taxied on the runway, I removed my ticket from the pages and handed her the book.

"For me?"
"Yes, ma'am, it's yours."
"I couldn't...I just wanted to see what you were reading."
"It's okay. I'm done with it...It's *League of Denial*. A book about the NFL."
"Are you sure?"

"Yes, ma'am."

"Well, God bless you."

"Thank you. Enjoy the book...God bless you as well."

She had that motherly worry on her face. She meant well, but she was worried about me. Worried about other players and worried about the NFL.

I was worried as well. I didn't know what the reports would say about my body, but I now worried about my brain as well.

October 28, 2013-Initial evaluation by XX D.C. CCSP.
The player presents on this day for headaches, neck pain, low back pain, bilateral shoulder pain, bilateral hand and wrist pain, bilateral hip pain, bilateral knee pain, bilateral ankle pain and bilateral foot pain.

He also complains of chronic headaches due to multiple concussions in the past with loss of consciousness.

Diagnosis given was joint pain, joint stiffness, myospasm, Achilles tendonitis, cervical radiculopathy, cervicalgia, headache, lumbalgia, back pain, neck pain, lumbar radiculopathy, patellofemoral syndrome, plantar fasciitis, rotator cuff syndrome, tendinitis of the knee patella, and the notes are right upper extremity impairment as well as a left upper extremity impairment.

The right upper extremity impairment that was done for total upper extremity impairment of the right side was 15%, and a total whole person impairment of the the upper extremity right side was 9%.

Also, the left upper extremity impairment, total upper extremity impairment, left side is 18%. Total whole person impairment on the left side was 11%. Right lower extremity impairment and a total lower extremity impairment, right side is 32%. Total whole person impairment, lower extremity right side is 13%. Next is left lower extremity impairment. Total lower extremity impairment left side is 32% and total whole person impairment, lower extremity left side is 13%.

Next rating impairment due to cervical disorders was zero, as well as the thoracic spine injury. For lumbar spine injury it was 8%. So combined whole person impairment was 41%. Pain rating was a two and whole person impairment was that of 42%.

The doctor placed his hand on my knee, as I placed my head in my hands. He apologized, but it wasn't his fault. I was the one who wanted to know what was going on with my body.
We took physicals every year in the NFL—before the season and after. I always received an apple and a perfect score. I was "Fit to play Football." At what point were they going to tell me my body was breaking down? At what point were they going to treat me for my ailments?

At what point was I going to be looked at as a person and not a product? CTE wasn't the only thing the NFL was hiding. They're also hiding our medical histories. The team doctors have a responsibility to the teams that are employing them, not the pretend patients—the players. Our best interests are not at heart when we're thrown out onto the field time and time again. Each player has an expiration date on us and the NFL team and their physicians know exactly when that date is, unbeknownst to us. This isn't retirement, this is us walking the plank.

Retirement in the NFL is a joke. The NFL doesn't care about retired players and I'm calling them out on it. I'm not going to go soft and send a company email; I'm going full throttle. I'm about to blast the NFL. I just need to say the right things that will get them to feel me. To feel me they have to be able to listen to me. To listen to me, they have to hear me. Now, how am I going to get the NFL to hear me?

What am I upset about?

I'm upset that the NFL uses its players like a cheap plastic cup and throws us away without even caring if we make it into the recycle bin. I've heard about numerous million dollar funds going to former players, but I'm wondering which former players are getting these benefits. I'm wondering, what, besides money, are the players getting? I've been a former player for over a year, and the only thing I've received is a notice that my insurance will run out in five years.

Some welcoming party.

I've called the NFLPA at least twice a month over the last four months, with different inquiries. Aside from the first phone call, the others have been horrendous. It seems as though I call the number and a woman says, "Hold, Please."

Then she goes and takes her turn in Foosball, then returns to the phone and says, "This is [Blank}, How may I direct your call?" It's a never ending cycle. They're too busy doing news conferences to do what's best for the players. I know it may seem that I am exaggerating or overstating some things, but I just think it should be a lot easier. It's tough because I know the NFLPA is handcuffed by what the NFL's needs and wants are. The first three letters of the NFLPA are...

Yeah. Exactly.

The PA, as much as they may want to help, will always play second fiddle to the NFL's owners. As of today, when Players retire we need to unlock the DA Vinci Code before we can attain our benefits.
Benefits that are rightfully ours, but nonetheless, they are the needle thrown into a haystack. NFL Players are used to a schedule, and structure, but when we retire, that schedule and structure are no more. A simple Schedule of retirement "to-do's" would go a long way. I know they just formed the "Players Trust," but I feel as though that was a rushed attempt at combatting the issues I set forth on Twitter. Oh yeah, Twitter. Twitter had a rude awakening on the morning of October 31, 2013.

The day that I would be a Trending Topic.

32
DON'T DO THIS

"The best of you is the one who has the best character." A saying of our beloved Prophet Muhammad, peace and blessings be upon him, echoed in my head.

As a Muslim, my character is everything. I don't want to do anything that will negatively affect my character or the purity of my heart. Public cursing, ranting and raving are not ways to attain good character. I've spent my entire life trying to be a model citizen, a good example, and a role model. With 140 characters, I would most likely throw it all away. I weigh the pros and cons. If I don't speak up, more players will feel what I feel. More players' families will be left with unanswered questions. More children will grow up fatherless. As a Muslim I believe in Judgement Day. On Judgement Day before God, I will be judged by myself.

When I stand before God, and He asks me, "How did you use what I bestowed upon you?"

I want to make sure I can answer positively.

"I used everything You blessed me with for the betterment of myself, my family, and mankind."

I thought about when God would ask me, "What did you do with the voice that I gave you?"

What if I said, "God, I used my voice to speak. I liked getting my speaking engagements with healthy honorariums, first class travel and photo opportunities. I couldn't speak up on those issues which concerned me, or else I would have lost it all." NO! I felt in my soul God did not send me, Hamza Abdullah, to be ordinary. To conform. To be average. To fall in line. I felt He fashioned me a leader, and wanted me to lead.

As I imagine my future, I know that everything I set out to do, must be to please God. Even when I make mistakes, as I often do, I must right that wrong soon after.

"Follow up a bad deed, with a good one." That's what I'd do. I'd tweet my manifesto, then discuss in finer details my points and concerns later.

As I began to tweet, I got phone calls and texts from friends who represent every major news channel. These individuals know me and have known me for most of my career. They've interviewed me about my humble nature and mild mannered presence among the chaotic lifestyle of the NFL. They've also heard me speak and know that I'm not a foul mouth individual who possesses a vocabulary riddled with profane four letter words. Cursing doesn't mean a person is ignorant, but it definitely gives others reason to believe they are. I was taught by my father a very valuable lesson. He taught me that a person who curses has a limited vocabulary and should read to increase his vocabulary. I had been reading a lot lately and had tried to communicate in a professional manner, with no results.

Nothing gets a response quite like "~~Fuck~~ you."

33

THE LAST YARD

October 30, 2013

I returned from my Midwest trip stewing. That day was the worst day of my life. My thoughts were racing.

Why do I feel like this? Nothing is going right. I've tried to apply for graduate school, I've reached out to coaches I knew, but got nowhere. What's going on? Why aren't people calling me back? Why didn't the NFL tell me I was hurt? What am I going to do?

I went upstairs to my media room and isolated myself. I didn't want to be around my family in this volatile state. I didn't know what to do. I didn't have anyone to tell because I didn't know what was going on. I sat in the room all day. Alexa knew not to bother me when I was held up in the media room. My media room was equipped with leather chairs, two flat screen televisions and a whiteboard. The whiteboard dawned a plethora of my scribbles, thoughts, and goals:

Call Coach. Call my parents. Spend time with the children. Respond to emails.

Today, none of that was getting done. I couldn't fake being happy. I was miserable. I hadn't eaten, hadn't slept, and hadn't drank any water before I descended the stairs to find Alexa finally sitting down after a long day. Since I was MIA, she was all alone. She had to get our children ready for school, drop them off, pick them up, take them to soccer practice, help them with their homework, make dinner, give them their baths, read them stories, and put them to bed. We locked eyes, and she had that "we need to talk" face. I wasn't in the mood to talk, I just wanted some fresh air.

"Hamza. Can you come here?"
"Yeah. Just a minute."
"Where are you going?"
"Nowhere...Yes?"
"Hamza, I don't like you being up in that room all day."
"I had to do something."
"What'd you have to do?"
"I had some stuff to think about."
"Like what?"
"Just stuff. Stuff that's going on."
"I was thinking about stuff too. I don't like what's going on with us. We're not getting along, you're disappearing for long periods of time, and I'm getting worried."
"Don't worry about me, I'll be fine."
"I'm worrying about all of us. You, the children, me, our finances...Everything."
"Don't worry, *in shaa Allah*, I'll take care of it."
"I know, but...It's just that...I went to Nordstrom Rack, and I wanted to get a sweater, but I didn't buy it. I'm worried about our finances."
"You're worried about money? Don't worry about anything. I told you when we first got married that I would take care of you."

I began to feel hot inside and I could no longer contain my emotions. I began to yell.

"As long as I have two hands and two feet, I WILL PROVIDE!"
"Hamza, I know, I just..."
"No! We have money. Buy whatever you want. We haven't been splurging. We're good."
"Hamza..."
"No, No, No! I'm tired of this."

I stormed out the door, jumped in my car and drove off. I left Alexa speechless with tears in her eyes. I was also speechless with tears in my eyes.

What was I doing?

Where was I going?

I drove to the gas station, and as I filled up the tank, I opened up my Instagram and typed:
October 30, 2013, 10:11PM

I pray Allah forgives me for my shortcomings and my mistakes. I'm not perfect nor have I ever claimed to be. If I've wronged you in the past, please forgive me. Allah brings different people in our lives for a reason. I'm thankful for every person, obstacle and blessing. I love you for the sake of Allah. *Assalamu Alaikum.*

I wasn't sure if these would be my last words so I wanted them to encapsulate what I thought my life was about. I jumped back in my car and turned the radio up as loud as it could go. I weaved in and out of traffic. Driving dangerously pushing my car to the limit. I jumped on the 60 freeway heading east. Sixty, 70, 80, 90, 100 miles per hour. I look up and see a freeway sign:

Interstate 15 North

Las Vegas————246.

Vegas. Let's go! Why Vegas? I didn't know, but that's where I was going. As I sped up the 15, I could hear voices in my head. One voice is telling me to go home, another is telling me to go faster, and another is telling me I need payback. Payback from who?

The NFL.

They're the reason you're in this mess. They're the reason no one is calling you back. They're the reason your body is banged up. They're the reason Alexa feels the way she does. They're the reason for everything.

I squinched my face up and wiped it with my right hand, my left hand secured tightly on the steering wheel. I didn't want to slow down, but I don't want to drive faster because then I would bring more attention to my car.

I've already come this far, so I can't turn back.
I like the third voice.

Payback. Yeah. Let's get payback.
~~Fuck~~ the NFL.
Yeah. ~~Fuck~~ em. ~~Fuck~~ them. ~~Fuck~~ everyone associated with them.
They want me to kill myself.
If I kill myself, I'll never get payback.
I'll be silenced forever and they'll continue to ~~fuck~~ players after me.
It stops with me. I just don't know how to do it.

As I approached Vegas, I could see the bright lights. Lights, camera, ACTION!

I pulled up to the strip, drove up to the valet, and parked. I went right to the front desk.

"I need a suite."
"Yes, sir, all I need is your ID and a credit card."
"I don't want anyone to know I'm here. I'm paying cash."
"I'm sorry sir, but I can't..."
"Please. I don't want anyone to know I'm here. Please."
"Okay sir, I'll make sure your name is not on the list."
"Thank you."
"Here's the key to your room, the elevators are through the casino on the left."
"Thank you."
"Have a great stay."
"We'll see..."

As I walked through the casino, I saw girls in short skirts, hustlers, and old folks. This wasn't a place for me. Not a married Muslim father of three.

I opened the room to my suite and saw the Vegas strip out the window. It was lit up but nothing like it will be when I start my payback.

I'm tired as hell, so this payback is going to have to wait till the morning...

34
TWITTER TIRADE

I couldn't sleep that night. I tossed and turned in a strange bed, in a strange place. Alexa wasn't lying next to me. No one was. I was alone. I looked at the clock, it read 5:30 A.M. I began writing my script. The script slash manifesto. It began and ended the same way.

"~~Fuck~~ you NFL!"

I wrote up 50 tweets dedicated to the NFL.

Today they will hear my voice and respond.

After finishing my script I went downstairs to the breakfast bar. I ordered oatmeal and orange juice as I sat watching ESPN. I waited until 8 A.M. local time before I opened up my Twitter App. Sitting at a bar in Las Vegas, NV, I began a historic tongue lashing.

8:00 A.M. CST:

"@HamzaAbdullah21: ~~Fuck~~ you @NFL #NFL"
"@HamzaAbdullah21: ~~Fuck~~ you NFL for doing your former players the way you're doing em"
"@HamzaAbdullah21: ~~Fuck~~ you NFL for lying to these people and denying the fact that football causes brain damage"
"@HamzaAbdullah21: Every player understood the risks of playing football, and we did it, and would do it over again!"
"@HamzaAbdullah21: We just thought/assumed we would be taken care of after we were done."

"@HamzaAbdullah21: ~~Fuck~~ you NFL for denying players their benefits and making us go through all these ~~fucking~~ hoops"

"@HamzaAbdullah21: ~~Fuck~~ you NFL because you are the plantation and WE are the slaves!!! #IfYouThinkOtherwiseYouAreDelusional"

"@HamzaAbdullah21: ~~FUCK~~ you NFL for that slave trade you call the "NFL COMBINE," where you strip us of our manhood."

"@HamzaAbdullah21: ~~FUCK~~ you NFL for wanting players to kill themselves so you can show the "SLAVES" what life off the plantation is"

"@HamzaAbdullah21: There's a reason 80% of former players either go broke or get divorced within 5 years of leaving the game."

"@HamzaAbdullah21: It's not poor choices by the player, it's the ~~fucking~~ NFL loading the gun, and us pulling the trigger"

"@HamzaAbdullah21: ~~FUCK~~ you NFL for not taking care of player families."

"@HamzaAbdullah21: ~~FUCK~~ you NFL..."

This continued for almost an hour. I had enough. My phone started ringing, dinging, and vibrating. I couldn't control the notifications.

I began to get a pounding migraine. I dropped a twenty on the bar and staggered back to my room. I needed to lay down. I laid in the bed, tears in my eyes, wishing I could end it all. This isn't life. It just isn't. I looked at the pillow next to me. I imagined Alexa gazing into my eyes. I imagined our first anniversary. She was seven months pregnant and had that motherly glow. We were in the mountains of Colorado Springs at a resort, enjoying life. She had a clean white robe on looking like a million bucks. What I wouldn't give to go back to that. To a time when life was simple. When I was an active player in the NFL. When the toughest decision I had to make was if I wanted sugar or honey with my morning tea. There wasn't any sugar or tea. No smiles and no good times. It was over. My life was over.

At that moment I thought about my brother. Husain. He was an active player then, but someday he'd be a former player. If I were to kill myself, he may be inclined to do the same. I couldn't let that happen. I need to talk to him.

"Assalamu Alaikum."
"Wa alaikumu salaam. Hamza? Are you alright?"
"Yeah," I replied, though I was sobbing.
"Where are you?"

"I'm in Vegas, but I'm safe."
"I love you, Hamza. You know we love you?"
"Yeah...I know..."
"I just got tired..."
"I know, Hamza. I know. We'll take care of them. Just promise me you won't do anything."
"I won't."
"Okay."

I sniffled as I tried to compose myself.

"Hamza. I have to go to practice, but I wanted you to know I love you."
"I love you too, Husain. Have a great practice *in shaa Allah.*"

Click

PART TWO

I AM NOT ALONE

"I am like that little ant in the front of the line; a lot of other ants depend on me, and follow me."
—Muhammad Ali, *The Soul of a Butterfly*

35

UMMIE KNOWS BEST

I returned from Las Vegas fragmented. My mother and wife greeted me at the door as I fell into their arms. My Ummie spoke.

"*Assalamu Alaikum*, Hamza."
"*Wa alaikumu salam*, Ummie."
"You said what you had to say."
"Yes ma'am."
"You're Hamza...I named you Hamza for a reason."
"You did."
"Yes. Hamza Ibn Abdul-Muttalib, may Allah be pleased with him, was the Uncle of the Prophet Muhammad, peace be upon him."
"Yes...He was."
"Hamza, he stood up for the Prophet. He stood up against oppressors."
"He did?"
"Yes he did...And you're standing up against those who you feel are being oppressive."
"Yes ma'am, I am."
"Now that you've said that, are you okay?"
"Yes ma'am."
"Okay. I don't want you to hurt yourself or anyone else."
"I won't, Ummie."
"*In shaa Allah*."
"Ummie?"
"Yes, Hamza?"
"Can you take my two pistols to the police station? I don't want them in the house with me."

"Yes, I can son...Are they going to question me about them?"

"They shouldn't. They're legal and I have my permits and licenses for them."

"Okay, where are they?"

"I'll run up and get them."

"Okay, I'll take them now. I left Abu Shante at home and he needs his dialysis, so I have to leave now."

"Okay, Ummie. I'll get the guns."

"And Hamza..."

"Yes ma'am?"

"Keep making *duaa*. Ask Allah to make it easy on you."

"I will, *in shaa Allah*. Thank you, Ummie."

"I love you."

"I love you too, Ummie."

My mother left carrying a blue duffel bag holding a 9mm Beretta and Springfield XD Tactical .45 caliber, along with 250 rounds of ammunition. I didn't trust myself. I didn't want to snap and have lethal weapons in my home. I was already a lethal weapon. I laid in my bed that night asking for supreme guidance. I needed a direction. I needed a purpose. I needed a reason to continue living. My psychologist asked me if I ever thought about suicide.

I had.

She asked me if I had a plan.

I didn't.

She told me it's not abnormal to think about suicide. But I felt it should be for me. I'm Muslim. I'm married. I'm a father. I have parents who love me. I have siblings who love me, and I played in the NFL.

Suicide should be the furthest thing from my mind. Yet it wasn't. It was at the forefront of my mind. I prayed for a clear sign before I went to bed. A clear sign was exactly what I got.

36
MIKE & MIKE & MOTIVATION

I woke up and turned to ESPN 2. Mike & Mike in the Morning, a sports-talk radio show, was on. To my surprise, I was the topic of discussion. Mike Greenberg and Mike Golic make up the tandem that has become the voice of ESPN. Mike Golic is a retired NFL player. I turned up the volume and stood motionless as I listened to their reaction to my day on twitter.

The segment of the show was titled: Love It or Shove It

Greenberg: "...Let's do Love It or Shove It...Our very own Bubba will present a variety of the headlines of the sports day and we will determine whether we love them or we will tell him to shove them."

Bubba: "Hamza Abdullah rips the NFL and Roger Goodell on Twitter. Love it or Shove it?"

Golic: "...I say shove it…what are you doing?…There are issues…This is not even close to the way to go about it. You have just basically put yourself out there to say you have zero clue. You're a ranter and a raver. Have a discussion about it. Say something sensible without putting every swear word in front of it so you don't sound like a lunatic. That's my thought on that. You can have a discussion. You can have a very good discussion about it all. But the way he went about it. That's not going to do anything.

Greenberg: "...I think Hamza Abdullah…I don't know anything about Hamza Abdullah…I think he is doing his own case a disservice. One of the things I firmly believe in: "Sometimes the louder you yell, the less people hear you." ...While he is bringing up important and legitimate issues...in my opinion he is doing himself a disservice. By putting it the way he does...go to his twitter feed...every single one of them has the F word in capital letters...In my opinion, it detracts from the credibility of the rest of what he's saying."

Golic: "If you are this steadfastly against what's going on...What are you doing that's going to invoke change?"

Greenberg: "He's bringing up valid points...."

Golic: "These have all been brought up before, there's nothing new that he brought up in any of these tweets that hasn't been discussed before..."

Greenberg: "Yeah..."

Golic: "There's a little bit of, at least, a discussion...You can have a discussion...I get it...there is a discussion...I hope he is as thoughtful and smart a person as some people say he is. And I hope when discussions do happen...that he can be a part of the discussion and part of the solution instead of the problem...when I read all this... are you kidding me...he's not going to be part of the solution...and some of these thoughts, I just say how can you say that...topics are open to discussion and should be discussed."

Greenberg: "The louder you are, the less people will listen... *Reading a listeners email*: "From Ryan: You just gave Hamza Abdullah the entire top of the hour segment at eight o'clock, would you have done that without the language that he used. You had not even heard of him before this morning, and now you are directing people to his twitter account and discussing the issues he wants discussed. You may disapprove of the language he used but now your entire rush hour audience knows about him and he brought more light to the issues he finds important. I think he is the winner here."

"I started taking what he was writing a lot more seriously because I follow Jay Glazer from Fox on Twitter...

Another listener's email: "You told us that Jay Glazer is vouching for him...thus casting some validity on the things he's saying..."

"Maybe he did accomplish what he was trying to accomplish...It does make me wonder how many current/former NFL players feel that strongly about these issues..."

Mike Golic was right. There have been "discussions" about these issues. And they're still issues. Instead of sitting around discussing topics, it's time to enact change. Mike Greenberg was also right. It does make me wonder how many current/former NFL players feel that strongly about these issues.

There's only one way to find out. I would sit down and interview retired players and ask them about their transition and feelings towards the NFL. After interviewing them, I would write their stories in their own voices. I have changed their names, teams and/or positions to shield their identity. God willing, I have captured their true voice, feelings and story.

Here are the introductions to their stories.

37
RANDY:
GREEN BAY PACKERS WIDE RECEIVER

Randy was my first player interview, and I was a little nervous. I didn't know what to expect. I was anxious to see his reaction to the questions I had and if he'd be honest. I knew Randy from our playing days in the NFL. He was quiet as a church mouse. He randomly giggled, recalling an inside joke between him and himself, and he wasn't one to volunteer information. I'm surprised he even granted me the interview, but I told him I wanted to tell an unbiased account of what players go through when they transition from the NFL. On the flight to visit Randy, I wrote up some questions to guide the interview just in case we got hung up. I wanted the interview to flow, so I outlined some key questions that I felt would provide pertinent information to the players.

"Take me through your last game until now."
"~~Shit~~...Man, I haven't thought about that in a minute. Let me see..."
"Take your time."

He began to illustrate a story that sounded all too familiar to me. He didn't "fit" in the teams plan moving forward. I heard it all before. That was one of the recycled comments front office personnel and coaches use all too often. Then Randy dropped some knowledge on me, that I'm not sure I fully understood.

"Everyone goes through the same thing, but we will never tell anyone because we're competitors."
"What do you mean?"
"This Transition. This tough Transition."

135

"Explain. Please."

"We're competitive in every facet of this industry and it especially holds true when we're done playing."

"I see..."

"If someone is doing well, I can't show them I'm not transitioning as well. I can't have any regrets."

"Wow. That's deep."

"Yeah. That's why guys don't ask for help. In their minds they're still competing on that field."

"That's so true."

"They think they're winning, but in actuality, we're all losing."

"All of us?"

"Yes. Until someone stands up—someone famous, a superstar who says, 'I need help'—the cycle will continue."

"I never thought of it like that."

"That's just the way it is."

38
KEVIN:
MINNESOTA VIKINGS LINEBACKER

As I wrap up the interview with Kevin, I can't help but ask this burning question.

"Would you do it all over again?"

"~~Fuck~~ no."

"Haha. Really?"

"I wouldn't give them a day of my life again."

"You're the first player I ever heard say they wouldn't do it all over again."

"It's not a long term career. I'm not even 30 and I'm already on my second career."

"That's true."

"And it's the most physical sport, and we don't have guaranteed contracts."

"You're preaching to the choir."

"It takes away from your family time and you don't have time for anything else."

"That's another true statement."

"I look at the people I went to school with, and I feel so far behind."

"I never thought of it like that."

"And the NFL ain't helping."

"Nah, they're really not."

"They do stuff here and there, but it's just to get us out of their hair."

"Man…"

"We gotta change it."

"We sure do."

39
DARWIN:
SEATTLE SEAHAWKS SAFETY

I've been cut three times by NFL teams so I know exactly what Darwin was describing. Sitting at home watching all the games hoping someone gets hurt. What an awful wish to have, but it's our reality.

"The only way I can resume my career after getting cut, is someone going down with a significant injury."

Darwin said what every NFL street free agent has thought.

"We're like crabs in a bucket."
"We are?"
"Yeah. We need a guy to go down, in order to get back in."
"We dang sure do."
"I want the next man to succeed, but now I'm not looking at him like a brother."
"What are you looking at him like?"
"An opportunity."
"Dang. That's cold."
"It's our reality."
"That's a harsh reality."
"It's the NFL."

40
REGGIE:
INDIANAPOLIS COLTS DEFENSIVE END

Before sitting down with Reggie, I had only heard of depression in women who had just given birth, or in men who had lost their job. I never thought about it in relation to NFL players. Especially a behemoth of a man, like Reggie. He was the biggest guy I interviewed, yet the most open about his feelings and mental health.

"The first thing you need to know is that depression is real."

"Depression?"

"Yeah. Depression."

"What makes you say that?"

"You're hurt and you have a lot of things going on with you. You're going through things mentally that you can't even explain."

"That's true."

"It doesn't matter how big you are or how tough you think you are, you won't be able to get out of it."

"Dang."

"Depression manifests itself in so many ways."

"Like what?"

"Drinking, hanging out late, not being motivated, isolating yourself, womanizing..."

"You just diagnosed the entire NFL with depression."

He laughed, "Damn near."

"Seriously though. We never talk about stuff like this."

"And we won't. Our mindset has always been to fight through everything. But you can't fight through this."

"That's heavy."

"Indubitably."

41

CHARLES:
CLEVELAND BROWN TIGHT END

C harles has been a player I've respected from up close and afar. He was a starter since day one in the NFL and he always did his job. Everyone knew what they were going to get with Charles and that's exactly how the interview was going. Nothing in his story surprised me until he spoke about coaching.

"I used to want to be an NFL coach."
"Me too."
"I love the x's and o's."
"Who you telling?"
"But once you go behind the scenes and see how the coaches play games with peoples' lives..."
"Games?"
"Yeah. They play games with peoples' lives."
"How so?"
"They'll know they're going to cut a guy, but they string him along."
"Yeah. I've seen that."
"They ask him to do everything under the sun, and he does it. And does it right."
"Yep."
"But then, they'll find a way to say he messed up or did something wrong."
"I've seen that happen."
"They have his livelihood in their hands...They're going to cut him because someone upstairs doesn't like him or because they want someone cheaper."
"Hmmm..."

"I wouldn't be able to sleep at night. I wouldn't be able to live with myself, knowing I cut a guy who did everything I asked him to do."

"You got a point."

"Everything he's ever worked for is right there, and they're playing with his sanity, his family, and his career."

"Truer words have never been spoken."

"That's why I couldn't do it."

"When you put it like that, I couldn't do it either."

42
PATRICK:
MIAMI DOLPHINS RUNNING BACK

Patrick sat at the table with a straight face and spoke candidly about drugs in the NFL.

"I've never done HGH or Steroids, but I should have."

"Wait...What?"

"~~Fuck~~ yeah. If I would have known then what I know now, of ~~fucking~~ course."

"Why?"

"Why not?"

"It's cheating."

"So. All these ~~motherfuckers~~ getting big contracts after juicing. Why can't I get paid?"

"Not saying you can't get paid, but..."

"Man. I'd be an idiot not to juice."

"These cats are getting paid."

"Yep. They serve their little four game suspension, and it's back to cashing them checks."

"They are cashing them checks, though."

"Big checks."

43

TRAVIS:
SAN FRANCISCO 49ERS OFFENSIVE LINEMAN

There were times during the interview process I had to ask the player to repeat what he said, but Travis took the cake. Literally.

"I'm sorry you're going to have to repeat that one more time," I chuckled.

"Hamz, I promise you. There wasn't nothing like it."

"Nothing?"

"Nothing!"

"So the one thing you missed most in the NFL, wasn't the game, wasn't the money, wasn't the locker room, but the..."

"Yeah, Hamz! The Saturday night before the game at the hotel."

"Seriously?"

"Hamz, they had 15 different types of ice cream, cookies, cakes..."

"Haha. You can go buy ice cream right now."

"But it ain't the same."

"All I had to think about was football. I was so relaxed and free."

"They do take care of you."

"Yeah they do."

"I'm going to go out on a limb and say, you're the first and only player to miss the ice cream the most."

"Haha! Maybe, but that's what I miss the most."

"Only a Lineman would say something like that."

44

DEJUAN:
CHICAGO BEARS WIDE RECEIVER

Every NFL player will one day get cut, but I'm not sure they'll get cut like DeJuan. Before I could fully settle into our interview, Dejuan got right to it.

"They cut me over the phone."

"What do you mean?"

"I mean, they cut me over the phone."

"I don't get it."

"What don't you get?"

"How do you get cut over the phone?"

"I was sleeping in my hotel room at training camp, and the phone rang."

"I always hated getting calls on the hotel phone."

"Me too. So I hung it up."

"Then what?"

"Then they called again."

"What happened?"

"The dude told me don't hang up. We're releasing you today."

"Dang. He couldn't tell you we need to see you?"

"Nah. I guess they didn't want to see me again."

"Bro that's messed up."

"Tell me about it. They woke me up outta my sleep just to tell me I was cut."

"I just don't get why they would do that."

"Me neither. That's that ~~bullshit~~."

"That's the NFL."

45
SEAN:
BUFFALO BILLS QUARTERBACK

I assumed Sean would be the most well-off interviewee because he was a quarterback. I was sadly mistaken.

"I had to file unemployment three times."

"No way."

"I had to get up and go down to the office. I had just got fired from my job."

"How did you know to do that?"

"One of the other players who got cut told me to do it."

"I guess people don't really look at the NFL as a regular job."

"It is."

"Man. That's tough."

"Here I am with a college education, I played in the greatest league ever, and now I'm in the unemployment line."

"Talk about a change of scenery."

"And it's not like I can go in there unnoticed."

"Well, yeah, you're Sean. You were up for the Heisman trophy, and you were a star quarterback."

"And everyone in Buffalo knew me."

"Really?"

"Yeah. I caught people staring at me."

"Wow...really?"

"Yeah. And I'm like, what the ~~fuck~~ are you looking at?"

"Haha."

"Seriously. I'm like, what the ~~fuck~~ are you looking at?"

I chuckled again, the scene was hard to imagine.

"They're asking me dumb ~~ass~~ questions like, why are you here?"

"Uhhh..."

"Exactly. The same ~~fucking~~ reason you're here. Now get the ~~fuck~~ outta my face."

"Dang. I know that was tough."

"It was. It hurt my pride. I never took my wife or kids. I never wanted to put them through that."

"I don't think anyone would."

"People would say, you're a good looking dude, anyone would hire you, you just have to make some calls. I wanted to punch them in their ~~fucking~~ face when they said that."

"Uh, hello..."

"Exactly. I'm like, don't you think I've made every call, sent every email? I've tried."

"Some people just don't get it."

"Well they'll get it now after reading this..."

"They'll have no choice..."

46

RAMONE:
DALLAS COWBOYS CORNERBACK

As I sat across the table from Ramone, I had a hard time believing what he was saying. I didn't think he was lying, I just couldn't believe what he was saying.

"The dope game was my transition plan. I was making $15,000 a month. Easy."

"Easy?"

"It was easier than backpedaling."

"And you can backpedal in your sleep."

"I was pulling up in different cars every day."

"Dang. Like that?"

"Just like that."

"How?"

"I would put up half of the front money, and my boy would put up the other half."

"For what?"

"Crack Cocaine."

"Dang."

"It was all profit too."

"But you were a full time football player."

"And a part time drug dealer."

"You couldn't have thought that would last."

"I did. I thought I was smarter than the cops."

"I'm sure everyone thinks they are."

"You right. But I couldn't see working that hard playing football when I could flip four or five keys and I'd have a season's salary."

"Man, that's dangerous."

"It is, but it's high risk and high reward."

"I say all risk."

"Maybe, but I took care of all my people...I treated my team well. I was the Jerry Jones of the streets...They were all rewarded."

"I'm sure they don't see serving time as a reward."

"When you put it like that, you're right...I don't either."

PART THREE

LETTING GO, NOT GIVING UP

"...after hardship, God will bring ease."
—Qur'an, Surah 65 Ayah 7

47

LESSONS LEARNED

After sitting down with the players, I realized the magnitude of this book. This is the story these individuals have held inside for far too long. They were afraid of disclosing their story for fear of the reaction. I'm surprised at the level of honesty and detail they offered me. I'm not a complete stranger, but I'm pretty close to it. My saving grace is I'm a retired NFL player, just like them. They confide in me. They tell me things I know they've never told anyone else.

I can see the weight lifted off their shoulders as they speak. An hour turns into two, and sometimes three. It's therapeutic for these players to finally be able to tell their story. It's therapeutic for me writing it. It's tough to sit back and hear big strong men talk about being vulnerable and alone. I want to go across the table, give them a hug and tell them they have a brother in me, but I can't. Not now. I'm Hamza the writer, not Hamza the counselor.

I began asking questions throughout the interviews, but I found that approach to be menacing and interruptive. What worked best was me typing and the players talking. These players talked of sex, drugs, money, guns, divorce, jail and violence without batting an eye. They were comfortable telling me their stories, and I want to make sure I represent them the right way. I was able to sit down with these individuals and get their stories because they trusted me to do right by them. To afford them anonymity while still sharing their experiences. Their real stories that they are living, have lived, and will live going forward.

I initially planned to include the players' full stories in this book but I wanted to give their stories the attention they deserved. With their stories sandwiched by my story, I was afraid my story would overshadow theirs.

151

That's not what I want. These players' testimonies play a major part in fixing the transition system. Therefore I have decided to compile their stories in a follow-up book to this one titled:

NFL Players: Following Hamza Abdullah
As I put the finishing touches on these interviews, I begin to self-reflect.

"Where am I in my transition? Am I helping or hurting myself?"

While sitting with Sean, I wondered what the first step to a successful transition was, and it hit me. I'll never get to the fast lane of life, if I refuse to merge from the slow lane. I have to retire. I have to stand up in a room of anonymous individuals, and state my peace.

"Hi everyone. My name is Hamza."
"Hi, HAMZA!"
"My name is Hamza, and I am retiring from the National Football League." The group of anonymous individuals claps and cheers.

There, I did it. I'm free. I no longer have to wait for that "call" to come. I no longer have to move my family from short-term lease apartment to short-term lease apartment. I no longer have to push through a grueling workout because I'm going back to the league. I no longer have to check NFL.com to see the other safeties—not named Hamza Abdullah—signing contracts with NFL teams. I no longer have to make an excuse as to why I'm in Los Angeles on Sunday, and not on an NFL playing field. Nope. I'm done. Retired. The first step to a great transition, is leaving your past in the past.

"It's called the past, because we're getting past."

Thank you Ms. Alicia Keys for those *Lessons Learned*. It suits the transition well.

48

RETIREMENT

I officially announced my retirement on December 6th, 2013. I'm not a big star, and didn't play for one organization for the duration of my career, so a press conference was not necessary. A simple post on my social media pages did the trick. I used a picture from a preseason game in 2006 when I played for the Denver Broncos as my backdrop. That night we played against Star Rookie Quarterback Vince Young and the Tennessee Titans. I had a great game, and even tracked down one of Young's deep passes over the middle, for a diving interception. The picture I posted was of myself immediately after the interception; a smiling Denver Broncos number 21, football in my left hand, chinstrap secured tightly, white half sleeves on my arms, tape on my cleats, and my orange mouthpiece showing. I was smiling from ear to ear. As much joy as I felt that day, I felt a sense of sorrow reliving it. I ended my NFL career with zero interceptions during the regular season. I had plenty in practice and preseason games, but those don't count. They don't count according to the NFL, but they count to me. I did it. I played in the NFL. And on this Friday morning in early December, I'm calling it a career. The message was simple and to the point. I wrote:

After 7 years in the NFL, I've decided to retire and move on to the next chapter in my life. I was fortunate to play football at it's highest level, and will forever be grateful to the individuals who aided me along my journey. I only played one year of varsity football, started one year in college, and was a 7th round draft pick. I wasn't supposed to make it 7 years, but it was not my plan. It was Allah's plan. Allah plans and man plans, but surely Allah is the best of planners. Thank you to my wonderful family, friends, teammates and coaches. I truly appreciate the outpouring of support for Husain and myself. God willing, I will continue to be a positive influence

and example for change. Change for the better. Allah has blessed me with a voice and a platform, which I intend to use. I want to promote equality, tolerance, and of course "Wanting for your brother, what you want for yourself."
Please continue to keep me and my family in your prayers, as I will try and do the same. Peace and blessings to all. — Hamza Abdullah

I did it. I played in the NFL, and now, I have retired from the NFL. I had been waiting to exhale for years. Now was the time to take a break, then get back to the grind. It's a different grind, but it's still a grind. I think about life in five years...10 years...20 years and beyond. I think about what my body has been through and what I'll go through moving forward. I have already been told I will need a knee replacement within the next 10 years. I wonder what other ailments I may suffer during the next few years. I am only a few years removed from the game, and have played in less than 100 NFL games. I wonder about my buddies that started and played in nearly every game of their NFL careers. All the practices they participated in, and what their bodies must feel like every morning.

I am fortunate and blessed to have been spared a multitude of the pounding and collisions of the NFL game. During my career, I would be incensed whenever I was passed over as the starter, and relegated to backup duty. Now, I thank God that I didn't participate as much as I wanted to. As tough as it is to get out of bed now, I couldn't imagine what it would be like with a few more seasons or a few more games of wear and tear. I reached out to the NFLPA again, and applied for the LOD. With my physical exam reports, impairment rating and application in tow, I sent it off to the NFL office, where of course, I was denied.

"On January 14, 2014 the Disability Initial Claims Committee of the Bert Bell/Pete Rozelle NFL Player Retirement Plan considered your application for line-of-duty ("LOD") disability benefits. We regret to inform you that the Committee denied your application for LOD benefits."

According to the "Committee," I did not meet the requirement of having a 25% or greater whole body impairment. According to the report done by the Physician in Chicago, I had a 42% whole body impairment. The NFL's not so "neutral" doctor, found my whole body impairment to be 20%.

It must have been one percentage point for every minute I spent in his office. My doctor's appointment in Chicago spanned two days, and included x-rays, cat scans and MRI's of my entire body. The NFL's "neutral" doctor didn't do as much as snap a photo of me with his camera phone. The doctor visit was a joke, and my fate was sealed. I knew for sure I would be denied. Alexa pointed out the fact that when I was asked how I felt on the day of the physical, I said I was only a two on a pain scale of 1-10. With 10 being in severe pain. She told me that I had to wipe all previous doctor visits out of my mind. She was right. I have told doctors I was okay, my entire playing career.

The question was always, "Can you play football?"

My answer was always, "Yes." If I would have ever said "no," I would have cut myself. Yes, on a football players scale I was a two out of ten, but on a civilian's scale I was an eight or nine out of ten. I asked myself, "Does all this really matter?" Is the NFL asking me to help me, or do they have an ulterior motive. I think this whole process is backwards. Upon retirement, every player should be awarded the LOD benefit. They should also be given a thorough exam that lists and details every injury. They should then be linked with a healthcare network of orthopedists, chiropractors, physical therapists, counselors, and psychologists near their locale. All of this should be covered by the NFL and their insurance.

This would ease the players into transition rather than throw us out like yesterday's trash. It hurts us to wake up on the curb next to smelly garbage cans and unwanted electronics. We're not only hurt physically, but emotionally as well. I cry more often now than I have my entire life. I haven't cried this much since January 6th 2007. The day my teammate and beloved friend Darrent was laid to rest. I miss Darrent and will forever cherish the friendship we had. He was a dreamer and a thinker—like myself—so we got along very well. When I think of him, I think of his smile, and how infectious his positive personality was. I wonder what he would say if he saw me cry now. He'd probably tell me it would get better, then end the sentence with, "Already." Meaning, it's "Already" done. What is supposed to happen will happen when it's supposed to happen. There is no use crying over it. Already. I know this, and I believe this, but I can't help but tear up sometimes. I don't think it's a sign of weakness, I think something is internally wrong with me.

I need help.

49
THE TALK II

How many times have we heard the phrase, "I pulled myself up by my own bootstraps." I realize they might have pulled themselves up by their own bootstraps, but someone gave them the boots. A human being is not meant to be alone. We long for companionship. We need others around us. We also need a leader or a guide. Someone who has done it before. Someone that we trust.

A mentor.

I am very fortunate to have played with some quality individuals. They didn't hesitate to show me the ropes on the playing field, and now that I'm retired, they lend a hand off the playing field. Retirement brought more questions than answers. My schedule was going well, but my body hurt more and more. I could no longer lift weights like an Olympic weightlifter or run like I'm in Pamplona with bulls chasing me. My workouts had become lighter and shorter. It got tougher and tougher to get out of bed in the morning. My schedule was in danger of erupting, so I reached out to a former college teammate, and NFL veteran of seven years, Devard Darling. Every man gets "The Talk" by their father, older brother, or male role model when they're transitioning from boyhood to manhood. Devard was preparing to give me "The Talk II." There will be no *Birds* nor *Bees* discussed, just lower backs and knees.

He sat me down and explained to me that I could no longer wear basketball shorts under my jeans, just in case a basketball game broke out. I could no longer get designs cut into my hair at the barbershop. I could no longer laugh after passing gas. I would be the guy who led every sentence with, "Back in my day..." It was a tough pill to swallow, but I forced it down with a tall glass of truth juice. The truth is the truth, regardless of its messenger. Devard sent a clear message. Things are different now.

"H gunner, wass the deal?" Devard said with his Bahamian accent.
"Just cooling, D. Trying to get right before I get left."
"Yes sir. Yes sir. What you doing now?"
"Just trying to figure out what to do next. It's tougher than I expected."
"Don't trip, brotha. It's like that for everyone."
"I keep hearing that."
"Yes sir. We been doing this for ages, and now all of a sudden, we can't!"
"Yeah...All of a sudden."
"And what's the league doing about it?"
"Nothing!"
"Exactly. We have to do it for ourselves, bro."
"That's what I'm finding out."
"I know you been through a lot, bro, and people know you're frustrated, bro, but you have to keep getting better. It's good you announced your retirement because that's the first thing you have to do."
"That's what I'm learning."
"One of my boys went as far as to bury his cleats."
"Are you serious?"
"Yes sir. The boy buried his cleats."
"Wow. He wasn't playing any games."
"Not anymore. He had been working out trying to go back to the league, but it wasn't happening."
"I been there before."
"And he knew the only way to stop working out and living that lie, was to kill the player inside of him."
"Wow."
"I mean, it's a little extreme, but you get the point."
"Man that's deep. I've given most of my cleats away, so maybe subconsciously I'm doing the same thing."
"Maybe. Are you straight? Family good?"
"We're getting better, bro. Every day is a new test."
"Just take your time with it, bro. Make sure you check out that list of professionals I sent you."
"I will, bro. Thanks for the call."
"Of course, bro. I'm here for you. Hit me up anytime."
"Peace."

Included in this message were ways to get over my new ailments as well as receive my benefits.

He told me about workers compensation, physical therapy, and counseling. I began the conversation thinking Devard was another doubter I would have to prove wrong, but by the end of the conversation, I realized he was in my corner giving me key instructions to win the round as if he were Constantino Cus D'Amato. I would need every key piece of advice if I were going to not only win the round, but ultimately win the fight. I'm thankful I was able to reach out to someone who had been there and experienced what I am now struggling with. The transition is real, and just like a Captain in control of his ship, he is nothing without an experienced navigator.

50
SUICIDE

One thing Devard eluded to was alone time. He wanted me to be careful of my alone time. At first I didn't understand what he was getting at, but it soon became crystal clear.

Suicide.

Suicidal thoughts are not uncommon, but the urge to act on it frightens me. I fight this feeling and these urges, but it is not easy. Whenever I begin to think of suicide, I become reclusive. I don't want to worry Alexa, get into an argument with her, or say something that pushes her away. I know I don't want to die, but these thoughts are persistent. I begin to pray and ask God to forgive me for these dangerous thoughts and ask Him for guidance. A thought pops into my head to research suicide. I pull out my laptop and Google "suicidal thoughts." The first thing that pops up is a suicide helpline I can call. Right underneath the hotline is a link to a website that says:

"Suicide: Read This First."

I click on the link and the first thing the author asks is that I read this page in its entirety. I make the virtual agreement, and begin to read. There's a big statement in red that reads: "Suicide is not chosen; it happens when pain exceeds resources for coping with pain." What a profound statement. Some days I feel as though I'm in more pain than anyone on the planet. I know that's impossible, but my mind is telling me it's true. I continue to read, and the author advises me to do two things: (1) find a way to reduce my pain and (2) find a way to increase my coping resources.

I promise myself and the author to accomplish both of these tasks. I promise to look for a psychiatrist that can help me increase my coping resources as well as identify what makes me happy. As I scroll down to the end of the page I notice something that startles me. I burst into tears.

I notice the number of visitors this page has: 19,844,741!!!

Nearly 20 million people have read this. You're telling me that 20 million people have felt like this? What does this say about our society and our world? It's a bit hypocritical of me to look at this staggering number and feel as though I can help. How can I help them, if I can't help myself? I will help myself. I realize many of my problems begin with me comparing myself and my feelings and even my accomplishments to others. Comparisons are one of the most dangerous habits we can partake in as human beings. In the United States of America we're always comparing ourselves to someone higher than us. Be it professionally, intellectually, socially, economically, spiritually and even aesthetically. Comparisons are supposed to breed competition, but often times they create incompetence. We have to change this formula, and begin to look at those less fortunate than us.

There is a poem that says: "I cried because I had no shoes, until I met a man with no feet."

Life is about perspective, and we have to be careful not to teeter too far right or left. One day after researching suicide, I walked into one of my doctor visits to explain my physical ailments. To my surprise, the doctor flipped the script and asked me about my mental ailments. I told her I had suicidal thoughts, and she told me her husband committed suicide 15 years earlier.

My jaw dropped.

I felt the pain of her statement, and her situation. It had been 15 years, and she still carries that weight and burden with her.
I looked at Alexa, who was sitting next to me, and had a silent confirmation. In that moment, we realized we didn't want that to be us. I pray to God, that I do not inflict that pain on Alexa or anyone else that loves me. When I'm in that hole, it's tough to see or think about others. I feel so isolated and ostracized. I imagine myself waving my hands for help in the middle of the ocean. I think I'm drowning and no one wants to help me.

The reality is I'm not in the middle of the ocean; I'm in a swimming pool where the water is only three feet deep. I just need to listen to the lifeguard on duty and stand up. Instead of focusing on what I've lost, I promise to focus on what I've gained. Since I left the NFL, we've welcomed Maryam to our family, and Alexa is pregnant again.

All praises are due to God.

I know everyone's circumstances are different, as are their feelings. I won't dare say a person's negative thoughts are not justified nor will I be dismissive of them. I do believe there are certain people in our lives that we can truly confide in, that really have our best interest at heart. I recommend strengthening those relationships. For me, that person is Alexa. She makes me happy, and she is always there to listen. She reduces my pain, and supplies me with a coping resource. The two keys to uplift me out of my suicidal hole.

Alexa reminds me to lean on my relationship with God, because He's always there for me. She reminds me of a verse in the Qur'an.
Chapter 65 verse 7. The translation of the verse from Arabic to English, reads:

"...after hardship, God will bring ease."

Times are difficult now, but I believe, as I'm sure you believe, that it will get easier. If you're reading this promise me, that you will remember this verse. Whenever you're having a tough time, and there is no end in sight, remember this. I will surely try my hardest as well.

Not long after that doctor visit, suicide reared its ugly face again. Alexa and I were headed to San Diego for a doctor's evaluation related to my LOD benefit, when my cellphone began to buzz. My friend sent me a text message.

The message read:

"I need you. My brother committed suicide last night and I couldn't talk him down."

I was frozen after reading his message. I didn't know how to respond, or what to say, I just wanted to be there for him. I picked up my phone and called him. I had researched suicide and even contemplated it days before. Now here I am face to face with an actual event. I was ill prepared to console my friend, but I wanted him to know I was there for him. He spoke in a muddle that was hard to comprehend, and I wasn't going to push him. My heart sank as he eventually hung up to tend to more pressing matters. I said a prayer for my friend and his family, but wasn't satisfied. I asked myself, why is suicide glorified and thought to end all of our problems, when it does nothing of the sort. Suicide does not supply answers; rather, it leaves us with unanswered questions. Believing the world is a better place after suicide is a twisted assumption.

The night before my trip, I stumbled across a website where family members of suicide victims spoke candidly. One mother of a suicide victim spoke of the horrific scene of finding her son shortly after he took his life. She asserted that that image would be engrained in her mind for the rest of her life. Suicide is not the pleasant scene depicted in Hollywood movies or the Shakespearean play "Romeo and Juliet." The mess left after a suicide is not easily cleaned with household cleaning products.

Suicide often leaves scars so deep it takes generations to recover.
We as a society have a duty to our fellow brethren to be there for them during their time of need. We all go through some type of depression and despair, where solitude makes the most sense. We think we're the only ones going through a tough time, and if we seek help, we are not tough. We all know the quote and misinterpret it.

"Tough times don't last, tough people do." — Robert Schuller

The way tough people last, is by seeking help. By being honest with ourselves, we understand that we cannot go at it alone. We owe it to ourselves to investigate the best plan of action, to uplift ourselves. We also owe it to those closest to us to let them know when we're going through a troubling time.

I've been fortunate to have ex-teammates and friends who have been and are actively going through their transition, at the same time as me. Erik has pulled me out of the gutter on a few occasions, and I'm sure I have reciprocated that deed. Although we may not talk to a loved one, friend, or colleague on a daily basis, that does not mean, the love is not there. In our solitude, we listen to the whispers and we believe there's not a soul on earth that truly cares about us and our well-being. The devil is a lie.

There *are* people who care about us. If I died today, those same individuals who I thought did not care about me, would hop on a plane to pay their final respects. They would question themselves and wonder why they hadn't known. Why they couldn't see the signs, and why I did not reach out to them. I have a duty to let my loved ones know I am not doing well. This way, we can all come together to enact a better course of action, for my well-being. We must first take ownership and be proactive. I know that I am challenged mentally, so I will do my part to address this situation. I will read, research, and respond sincerely to those individuals inquiring about my health. My health is in my hands, and I am determined to live a healthy life.

I know that regardless of the number of books I read, the number of counseling sessions I sit in, and the number of people giving me positive words of encouragement, I will still have days where I doubt myself. I will still have days where that true happiness eludes me, and I will search for answers. Although I may not get the answers I want or need, I will pursue happiness.

Happiness permeates from within. True happiness that is.

True happiness will not come in the way of a retail purchase, a compliment from a total stranger, or the belittling of others. True happiness will come when I am honest with myself, and I focus on those things I can control. "Let go and let God," as my church going friend once told me. I will focus on myself and pray about those things I cannot control.

Deepak Chopra, in his book of enlightenment *The Ultimate Happiness Prescription*, has seven points that we can all benefit from.

1. Declutter your surroundings.
2. If you buy something, give something away.
3. Spend money to help the environment, returning a fraction of Nature's gifts to you.
4. Do something that's not for profit
5. Be generous
6. Be lavish in your giving, particularly with intangibles.
7. Nourish your body instead of defiling it.

I believe these points are of great benefit and coincide directly with what those who are going through a life transition would like to accomplish in the long run. I will try and abide by these points and pray that you can do the same.

51
LOOK UP

I came home from one of my out-of-town interviews and wanted to do something special for my family—so I made breakfast. I'm no five star chef, but I can follow simple directions. The Food Network website is the worst kept secret for people pretending they know how to cook. I looked up and found recipes for a Colorado omelet, apple buttermilk pancakes, and a strawberry cheesecake bread. I added my special breakfast potatoes, some fresh fruit and orange juice. Breakfast was a success. My children enjoyed it, but they wanted more. They didn't want more food, they wanted to spend more time with their oft-traveling father. I informed them we would go on a walk after I finished cleaning up the mess I made in the kitchen. After scrubbing pots, swabbing floors and disinfecting countertops, it was time for our walk.

We have a small red wagon that we use for trips to amusement parks and zoos that I pulled out of the garage. I placed Aqil and Maryam in the wagon, along with snacks and water bottles. The wagon seats two, so I allowed Layla and Aqil to rotate between walking with me and sitting with Maryam. As we embarked on our trek, I held Layla's hand in one hand, and the wagon in the other.

We set our sights on the 7 Eleven a mile down the road. As I walked briskly, I listened to my children's tales. They spoke about their time at the park the day before and eating pizza. Maryam sat back and enjoyed the ride, the passing pedestrians, and the cars that zoomed past. Halfway through the walk, Aqil asked if he could get out and walk, but I told him, "No."

I could only hold one of their hands while still pulling the wagon. I needed to be in control. I needed to control the pace and control them so they wouldn't dart out into the street or get too close to the curb. At around the same time, Layla began to say her legs were burning and hurting. I attributed her leg fatigue to poor physical education at school.

Surely when I was six, I was able to walk miles at a time without getting tired. I compromised, as we stopped for a hydration break.
After 30 seconds of water and rest, we had to get back on pace. We had to make our time. I'm not sure what time, but we had to make it. As we continued our journey, we passed an elderly couple. They loved seeing a father walking with his three children. I'm sure it took them back to the time when they were young and doing the same thing with their children. We waved and kept it moving.

It was a surprisingly warm day and I knew a thirst quenching drink would be a perfect end to our walk.

When I was a young boy, I loved going to 7 Eleven for an ice cold Slurpee. We pulled the wagon inside the store and began the delicate process of choosing Slurpee flavors. My children chose the same flavors I used to when I was their age. Cherry and blue raspberry mixed. We had reached our destination, and now it was time to head back home. I didn't want Aqil in the wagon with the drink, fearful of Maryam attacking him like a bear attacks campers on a picnic, so I allowed him to walk with Layla.

By this time, Layla had forgotten about her ailing legs. With drink in tow, my eldest two began leading the way back home. The wagon was much lighter now, with Aqil skipping and drinking with Layla. They were smiling and enjoying themselves, but I still wanted to keep up our pace. We raced to an intersection, where we sat and waited for the stoplight to change green.

"Green means go, and red means stop!" Aqil shouted proudly as we approached the crosswalk.

There was a bus stop adjacent to the stoplight, and on the bench sat three elders. Two men and a woman. The three elders smiled and waved at my children the entire time we stood and waited for the light to change. They thoroughly enjoyed my children. I sat back and observed what was happening, and a light went off in my head.

I told myself I needed to enjoy my children as much or more than total strangers.
I reached down to Maryam, still waving at her newly acquired admirers, and gave her a kiss and a snack. The light turned green, and we bid our elder friends adieu, as we crossed the street. Layla and Aqil were immersed in a deep conversation about how their Slurpees were now purple. They began to educate me on the primary and secondary colors.

"We began with blue and red, now we have purple." Layla recited.
"If we mixed red and white, we would get pink." Aqil countered.

It was fascinating to hear my children breaking down the intricacies of Slurpee flavors and colors.

At this time, I threw out our pace and time. I wanted them to enjoy this time, and I wanted to enjoy the time with them. I conceded that I would go as fast or as slow as they wanted to go. We began with a snail's pace. As we walked slower and slower, Aqil exclaimed, "Abu! Look at these beautiful flowers. They're blossoming!"

I looked up, and along our walk sat Pink Trumpet trees approximately 20 feet apart, all with beautiful pink flowers. I had driven by this street hundreds of times, and walked by it at least 10 times, but I never looked up. Aqil asked me if we could pick some for mommy. I knew that would brighten up Alexa's day. A day where she was able to sleep in, have breakfast in bed, peace and quiet for an hour and receive freshly picked flowers. At this moment the earlier light that went off in my head, exploded.

This walk mirrored my transition.

The two ends, the beginning and ending, were my home and 7 Eleven. I was focused on the destinations, but my children were focused on the journey. The transition was the middle. The walk. They wanted to take their time, enjoy the sights, sounds, and time with their father. I needed to take a page out of my children's book, and enjoy the now, instead of being absorbed in the pain of the past or the hope of the future.

As Aqil and Layla finished their Slurpees, they discarded their cups in nearby trash bins and began to run. They ran at such a pace, I couldn't keep up. I was still towing the wagon with Maryam. I wanted to scream for them to slow down and stop, but I agreed to move at their pace. After a minute of running, they relinquished the rabbit like pace and dropped to the more suitable pace of the turtle.

After a minute of the slow pace, they ramped it up again. This went on for about 1/2 mile. As we neared our home, they took refuge on a bus stop bench. When I finally caught up, they requested a snack and water. They understood this was the last point of relaxation before we made it back home. They sat swinging their feet, pointing out different color cars that drove by, and shapes of clouds. After their consumption of graham crackers and granola bars, they jumped up and resumed their quest. They began to jog home at a pace outstretching my legs. I smiled, and kept up as best I could.

When we returned home, they presented Alexa with her gift and said, "Mommy we had fun on our walk with Abu!"

My children taught me a very valuable lesson. In life, our birth date is our beginning and our death is our ending. The dash in the middle is our transition. We wouldn't speed walk to our death. We know it's coming. We're better off enjoying ourselves and our loved ones while we are able to. In life we need to slow down and look up, or we'll miss the beautiful flowers. I want to smell the flowers while I'm still here. I promise to slow down and look up during my transition. In our transition, there is an opportunity for enjoyment and ultimately, growth.

I came across a book that would help me see even clearer. It spoke of the growth we have an opportunity to experience after something bad happens to us.

Post Traumatic Stress Disorder or PTSD, is a type of anxiety disorder that occurs after one has gone through an extreme emotional trauma that involved the threat of injury or death.

It is commonly seen in war veterans.
As professional athletes and professional football players, we also have seen instances where PTSD comes into play.

The book I picked up was titled *PERSPECTIVE: The Calm Within The Storm* by Robert J. Wicks. In his work, Dr. Wicks opens up the door to Post Traumatic Growth or PTG. PTG refers to positive psychological change experienced as a result of the struggle with highly challenging life circumstances.

Dr. Wicks writes:

"...when post traumatic growth occurs, we begin to appreciate that it is not the amount of darkness in the world that matters. It is not even the amount of darkness in ourselves that matters. In the end, it is how we stand in that darkness that is of the essence."

In order to fully appreciate this transition phase that we're in, we must first try not to defeat it. The Transition cannot be beat, because it is not a game. It's the end of a game, and the beginning of living. The Transition is Undefeated, and will remain undefeated as long as I and my contemporaries continue to wage war against it. I have waved the white flag and thrown in the ceremonial towel. I will no longer fight with my Transition. Instead, I will sit back and ride on this road of Transition. William Bridges, in his book *The Way of Transition*, explains the transition we experience as the dreaded Neutral Zone.

As an NFL defender, I was raised from an early age to never venture into the neutral zone because it would precipitate an offsides penalty on myself. There are no more penalty flags, thus no more football rules I need to abide by. Just the rules of life. This is my life. This is my Transition. I've come to grips that my NFL career is over, but my life is just beginning. I will embrace this Neutral Zone and use it as an opportunity for growth.

I'm not worried about my destination or my ETA, I'll get there when I'm supposed to get there.

52

FORGIVENESS

I highly recommend a form of prayer or meditation as soon as you wake up in the morning. It relaxes the body and centers the soul. It's a mental and physical warm up, that will ensure you are ready for the biggest day of your life.

Today.

I live for today, and I live for my Transition. My Transition is just that, mine. I had been searching for outside influences and outside pleasures for an inner fulfillment. I found it buried deep inside of me. The will to be healthy. The will to be successful. The will to be able again. I still have bouts with episodic depression as well as lingering pain in my extremities, but my attitude is different. There will be no pity party thrown anymore. I am in control of my circle, my Transition, and my life. I was a victim of my mind, but I was led to believe I was a victim of circumstance. A victim of the NFL's massive health cover-up. My spectacles of sorrow were set on the NFL and getting even. I blamed the NFL for the shortcomings of myself and my comrades, but how can I or anyone else blame someone else for our own actions.

The NFL did not pull the trigger in these player suicides. If that had been the case, it wouldn't be deemed a suicide; it would be ruled a homicide. We can debate the circumstances surrounding these player suicides and what causes them, but to absolve the player would be unsophisticated. These players wanted us to learn from their suicides.

I will.

I have learned. The root of the problem is not in technological advances in football equipment. It's not in curtailing new rules for the field of play. It's not even in making more money. The problem is deeply rooted inside us all. The problem is that we lie to ourselves and believe we are alone.

We think we are the only ones going through a transition. We think we are the only ones experiencing difficulties. We think we are the only ones that care about our well-being. The truth is we are not alone, and we must declare war on that lie. We declare war on the voice that lies to us and tells us we are alone. The beauty of this problem, is that the solution lies right next to it. The solution of self-awareness and self-esteem. We cannot buy or borrow what comes from within. Self-esteem is what will blitz the problem and ensure that play is never ran again. The play of self-pity, self-alienation, and self-abasement. After we sack this feeling, we come to the Super Bowl of our soul, and that is Self-Actualization. It is here that we will find true happiness.

This was the lesson I learned from my fallen comrades.

They didn't want others to follow in their footsteps, but to create their own path. Create a path to truth. The path to Transition. The path to Transition begins with a whole hearted forgiveness. As we retire from our past relationship or work, we sometimes carry with us unnecessary baggage. I am not afraid to admit that I held strong resentment toward the League that I dedicated my life to. This unnecessary baggage can sometimes consist of anger, resentment, and bitterness. In our transition, we need to substitute these feelings with feelings of love and benevolence. Dr. Robert D. Enright discusses the healing process in his book *Forgiveness Is a Choice*. In it he writes:

"Unforgiveness, bitterness, resentment, and anger are like the four walls of a prison cell. Forgiveness is the key that opens the door and lets you out of that cell."

I, like many other NFL Players, felt unjustly hurt by the National Football League. We allowed anger and bitterness to overtake our mind and body, which resulted in the incarceration of our soul.

By being angry and showing public and private acts of resentment, we were only hurting ourselves. The NFL doesn't have time to worry about a player who doesn't like them. It's in our best interest, and the best interest of our health and Transition, to move on.

The truth can only be buried for so long, before inquiring minds begin to sniff it out. The NFL will have its day in court, but for my own safety and sanity, I will focus on what I can control. Forgiveness will uplift you out of that first road block of depression.

I have witnessed what forgiveness has done in my Transition, and I ponder on the effects it can have on others. I have forgiven the NFL and all those who I felt may have wronged me in the past.

More importantly, I have forgiven myself.

During my Transition, I blamed myself for my career shortcomings and other misdeeds. I was my harshest critic and lived in a guilty silo. I now understand that my NFL career had to go the way it did, or else I would not have had the passion, content, or time to write this story. I am at peace with my NFL career and myself. I enjoyed my time in the NFL, and I will cherish the relationships of my NFL peers. As an NFL player, there is nothing more rewarding than having the respect of your peers. I believe my peers respected me because I stood up for what I believed in.

I, like many other players, wanted to be the best player at my position. I wanted to be the highest paid safety, set the NFL record for interceptions, and have my jersey retired on the way to a Hall Of Fame career. Well that was my plan, but God had a different plan. God's plan was that I would introduce Islam to a demographic that may not have known about it before I came around.

I pray that I have done an admirable job at promulgating the message of Islam and letting people know that Muslims are people too.

53

ABU SHANTE

My family converged on Kansas City, MO for the final game of the 2016 season. This game would also be Husain's final game in the NFL—concluding his own seven year NFL career. The Chiefs were playing their division rival, Oakland Raiders. I had a feeling something special would happen that weekend, but I was not prepared for what happened on Saturday, January 2nd, 2016. After returning home from dialysis, Abu Shante went to sleep, and never woke up.

He was 55 years old.

He was surrounded by his wife, children, and grand-children. The standard questions began to arise, but then they all went away. Sitting on the floor in the hotel conference room, it hit me. The decision Husain and I made on March 20th, 2012, finally made sense. That was the day we announced we were leaving the NFL to go for our Hajj pilgrimage. Now here we are nearly four years later, and I got the clarity I was looking for. I had a conversation with myself about the man who raised me, molded me, guided me, and loved me...

May Allah have mercy on Abu Shante. The man who raised me to be a man...now Allah has called him home.

Yeah. Abu Shante was a man's man.

Where would I be if it weren't for Abu Shante?

Probably some scared little punk in a cycle of abuse.

Why would a man marry a woman who already had six children?

I'm not sure, but I'm glad he did.

He always said, "Hamza, someone's going to pay you to stay in shape." And he was right!

He believed in two things. Being a Muslim and being a hustler.

You ain't never lied. Abu Shante wasn't going to let anyone talk him out of Islam or outwork him.

And now we have to be those same hustlers and pillars of faith.

Yeah we do.

I can't believe he's gone.

Me either. But guess what?

What?

He's a Hajji!

A Hajji?

Yes. A Hajji! You guys took him to Hajj with you in 2012.

We sure did didn't we?

Yep. You did. And now he can rest in peace knowing that he completed all five pillars of his faith.

That last pillar is the toughest pillar. Not everyone can afford to travel to Mecca.

You're right. And Allah blessed you guys with the means and you spent it on your parents' pilgrimage.

We did, didn't we?

You did.

I didn't even think about that.
Alhamdulillah. All praises are due to God. So don't cry or worry about Abu Shante. He's good.

So that's why we had to make Hajj at that time?

Yep.

Wow. How selfish was I? I only thought about myself, my money, and my stature.

Don't be so hard on yourself. You didn't know.

I didn't know, but I'm glad I have a brother in Husain, who is wise beyond his years.

Alhamdulillah. Allah strengthened you with a companion like yourself.

Alhamdulillah. It all makes sense now. We are Hajji's. Abu Shante is a Hajji.

Yes he is.

May Allah have mercy on Hajji Abu Shante and all the Hajji's who have passed away.

Ameen.

54

CONCUSSIONS

There's a new book and movie, featuring Megastar Will Smith, aptly titled *Concussion*. *Concussion*, written by Jeanne Marie Laskas, focuses on the individual responsible for discovering CTE— Bennet Omalu. Omalu, a forensic pathologist, discovered CTE while conducting an autopsy on Pittsburgh Steeler great Mike Webster. What should have been a routine autopsy turned into a discovery that would have major ramifications in NFL circles. Omalu determined that Mike Webster died from repetitive blows to his head during his football career. A statement the NFL continues to deny and fight till this day. They won't be able to deny it for much longer because as more retired players die, they'll most likely have their brains examined. And as those numbers of players diagnosed with CTE increase, so will the heat under the chair of the NFL.

I've had my fair share of concussions, as I'm sure has every football player who's ever played the game. Football and concussions go hand and hand like basketball and sprained ankles.
Eventually it's going to catch up with you. Sadly, the NFL has treated concussions like a sprained ankle. We were told to, "Jog it off." We can't go back, but we can move forward. CTE is the buzzword on everyone's mind right now, but I'm not focused on it. I'm focused on treating the players' ailments and symptoms as they arise. Treating depression, anxiety, and stress. Offering players alternatives to prescription drugs and handguns.

In the NFL we are told the game is 90% mental and 10% physical yet we don't spend time on our mental health. We have a physical strength coach but don't have mental strength coaches. I'm changing that. I have started sitting down with a mental strength coach and I can tell the difference. My mental strength coach is certified in homeopathic healing and he happens to be my older brother, Abbas. His company, Be.Live, has helped me and others like me during our transition. It has helped unearth what players really want.

Players want to be a part of the NFL forever. They've earned that right, and it's time we gave it to them. I pray the discussions lead to the application of the solutions presented in those discussions. I also pray that retired players with a voice and platform remain truthful and forthright with themselves, the public, and other players. I will remain truthful with myself and with you. I miss being around the game, and I still have the itch to coach. I will resume my coaching inquiries in hopes I can find a situation where I can have a positive impact on young players.

55
MILITARY MINDED

I reached out to the coaches in my rolodex and asked about coaching. I got responses like:

"Reach out to every coach in your contact book and let them know you're interested in coaching..."

"Start at the highest level. It's easy to move down in this profession, it's nearly impossible to move up..."

"If you can get here in two weeks, I may have a job for you..."

These text messages filled my inbox after reaching out to the coaches in my phone book. The last message was from a coach at a big time school. I'm omitting his name, because I'm not sure if this is against NCAA rules. I immediately called him.

"What's up?"
"Hey, what's up Coach?"
"Are you finally going to come join me?"
"That's what I wanted to talk to you about."
"Well I'm here, and you know I want you to be a coach."
"Yes sir. I've always wanted to be a coach."
"And you're going to make a great one."
"Thanks, Coach."
"Are you still around town?"
"I'm not, Coach. I moved back to Cali to be near my parents."
"Smart man...I was hoping you were here."
"Yeah, I love it down there, Coach."

"And we loved you down here...well let me tell you what I was thinking."

"Alright, Coach."

"Well, we have our Graduate Assistants spots filled, but we may get one open in the spring."

"Okay."

"So I wanted you to come around the program, and get to know the guys and how we operate."

"That sounds awesome, Coach."

"Yeah, I want you to spend a year learning the process, then you'll be ready to go."

"I would love that Coach...the only thing is, my wife is pregnant."

"Congratulations, good for you guys."

"Thanks, Coach."

"Well, I don't want you flying back and forth..."

"So what are you thinking, Coach?"

"Let me work on this...I'll call you later."

"Thanks, Coach."

"Talk to you soon."

I agreed with the Coach. It would be beneficial for me to work around the school and get acquainted with the way of the program. Alexa agreed. She gave me her blessing and suggested I take the coach up on his offer. I was excited. I was going to get into coaching. I've always dreamt of being a coach, and I was finally going to get my shot. Then I thought about the players I interviewed and the others I speak to frequently. If I take a coaching job, I won't be able to continue this movement. This movement to change the system of the NFL. The movement to change the way players transition out of football. One day I want to be known as Coach Abdullah, but I won't make that commitment until I know there are no fallen soldiers I've left behind. My gym buddy Kevin, retired 15 year Army veteran, put it best:

"I'm glad you're okay...military minded; Never leave a man behind."

In shaa Allah, I will never leave a man behind.

56
WORDS OF WISDOM

I pray I have done my part in this equation by leaving behind some words of wisdom that I have learned along the way. I've learned that players run into trouble when we isolate ourselves. Whether it be perceived or palpable, players feel an increased feeling of paddling down a raging river on their own. Be it financial, physical, emotional, psychological, spiritual or mental, there is help out there for all of us that need it.

We've all heard the stories of divorce, bankruptcy, and suicide among former NFL Players. Without a clear direction, players are in danger of wandering those treacherous trails by themselves. When I began this journey, I wanted to come up with a way to eliminate these three disastrous endings to a Player's career and Transition. I understand there will be guys who get divorced or make bad investments and lose their money, but suicide is something we can't tolerate.

First we must recognize we are in need of help, then follow the steps to attain the proper help. I hope I can outline a blueprint to a successful Transition that can be the foundation for an improved life and lifestyle.

The steps to a smoother Transition were derived from my own experiences as well as the experiences of other players. There are a number of books written about transitions, forgiveness, and self-fulfillment, which I hope can work hand and hand with this book.

I truly believe if one were to follow these steps, that individual will be better prepared to identify the pitfalls associated with a tough transition.

The Steps to a smoother Transition are as follows:

Step 1- Officially Retire. You'll never move forward if you refuse to take a step forward.

Step 2- Take a Break. Get away from what you want to leave behind so you can see what lies ahead.

Step 3- Create a Transition Plan and Corresponding Schedule- You need to know where you're going and the proper steps to get there.

Step 4- Get a Mentor. You can't do this on your own. Enlist a trustworthy accomplice to accompany you on your journey.

Step 5- Evaluate Your Overall Health. You won't get very far if you're always on E.

Step 6- Control Your Circle. Family-Identity-Finances-Attitude.

Step 7- Write a Goodbye Letter. Once it's in the mail, the pain associated with it is gone forever.

I'm optimistic about my future, your future, and the future of our society. Mental health among men is not talked about as much as physical health is. I aim to change that beginning in the most macho and manliest of places; the football fields. Together we can make a difference. If anything in this book has helped you, please pass it along to someone else who may benefit.

CONCLUSION

I didn't think this day would come, but here it is. When I boarded the train of Transition, I didn't know my destination. I'm not there yet, but I am at a welcoming stop. I look up and the stop reads, "Author." I take pause with this station. Of all the things I would have imagined I'd be, an author is definitely not one of them.

I am the same guy who once turned in a four page paper with 237 words, 2.5 paragraph spacing and Courier New Font. I was able to manipulate my way through collegiate assignments, but this was different. I'm not sure who I thought I was kidding, my teachers were professors at an institution of higher learning and I was the stereotypical dumb jock trying to stay eligible. I was only kidding myself. I allowed myself to succumb to the way of the football world instead of carving my own path. I began my studies majoring in Engineering but graduated with a degree in Social Sciences. I allowed myself to take the easy way out. It wasn't until my senior year in college when I met Alexa and the prospect of having to transition earlier than originally thought, spurred me to take action.

That year I took History classes where I earned a 3.93 GPA, made the Presidents Honor Roll, and came four classes short of attaining a Bachelor of Arts in History. It was no coincidence that my transition from aloof student to Honor student happened when I met Alexa, who was also on the Honor Roll. She saw something in me that I didn't see in myself. I'm fortunate that the number one voice in my life, at that time and now, is a woman who believes in me and supports me. My pain has been reduced and my resources for dealing with that pain have increased. The scars of the game of football are still well entrenched on my body, but with every scar is a memory and a learning experience. With each scar I learned resolve and the ability to take my mind to places I never knew existed.

I need that resolve now more than ever. My battles on the NFL fields were tough, but nothing like the battle with the NFL to receive my medical benefits.

After an initial Denial of my benefits, I appealed the decision, and was sent to see another "neutral" doctor. This doctor took his time and gave me a thorough examination, and to my knowledge, identified me as a player worthy of the benefit. Apparently the NFL can't make up it's mind, as they've sent me another First Class form telling me I've been denied. I'm thankful and blessed that I am not in dire need, but I'm sure others are. It's a shame we must jump through so many hoops to get what's rightfully ours. Another hurdle that I'm aware of, and can plan for, during my Transition.

Between all the doctor visits I hadn't had the time to take a real break. I noticed Husain was visiting California to play the San Francisco 49ers. I decided to use that as an excuse to get away. Going to NFL games are somewhat difficult now that I'm retired. There are different roadblocks that I never thought about while I was an active player. The first roadblock is getting tickets. I can no longer tell the ticket representative how many I need and where I need them. I now have to go on the general fan websites and purchase tickets.

I no longer get to bypass traffic and pull right up to the stadium to have my car valeted. Now I must pay the $30-$50 Dollars to park in a remote lot and walk to the stadium. Once I enter the stadium, I'm no longer greeted with high-fives by the stadium workers and officials, nor am I wished good luck. Now, my entrance to the stadium is welcomed with boo's and "You suck," if I'm not wearing the correct team attire. I no longer get to walk into the double doors of an NFL Locker Room. One of the greatest feelings in the world is when the security guards open the doors and you see the team logo on the carpet in the locker room on gameday.

At that point, all the BS is worth it.

All the practices, the politics, the scrutiny, the sacrifices, the overcoming of obstacles, the doubters, and the heartache is all worth it. If I could bottle up that moment and save it, I would. It's the purest point of an NFL Players professional life. At that point it's not about the money, the fame, or the status. It's about achieving a childhood dream. I not only achieved, it but I maintained it.

I played for seven seasons and made it out relatively healthy. I'm thankful and blessed to have had the opportunity to be an active NFL player for as long as I did. I knew the end would come sooner rather than later, but it was still difficult.

I'm like a child who was breast fed but now my mother is weaning me off of her breast. The weaning never happened and I was cut off cold turkey. Not only did I not have a breast, I didn't have a bottle or replacement milk to nourish myself. Thankfully, I have a support system that understands I'll be delirious for a while. It'll take a while for me come to grips with what has happened but in the meantime they've set me up with tools to learn to feed myself.

The NFL has the formula, pun intended, but they're reluctant to offer it to its former players. Here I stand for all of my malnourished brothers who came before me and those that will possibly come after me.

Enough is enough.

NFL, move from in front of the door to a successful Transition and help us through it.

Stop denying guys their medical benefits. Stop denying that the injuries these players suffered while playing football were from playing football. Stop treating players like cheap goldfish. Stop lying to the public saying you are trying to make the game safer while strategizing behind closed doors on ways to minimize player benefits. Stop trying to end players' careers before they begin. Stop leaving players out in the woods to fend for themselves.

Start being the company that kids dream to work for. Start treating people as people instead of property. Start helping people become better individuals so that they may become better teammates. Start caring about the families of the individuals you hire and fire. Start giving a damn. Start by committing to the development of NFL players as people.

I've spent a lot of nights at this computer and I'll probably spend many more. I realize the Transition is not finite, but ongoing. I know some days will be better than others, but I pray this book serves as a road map and blueprint for myself and others. A blueprint to a smoother Transition. I'm thankful to have the opportunity to share my story and the story of other players with you the reader. I thank you from the bottom of my heart for reading this. I pray that this book is of benefit to myself, my family, yourself, your family, our community, this society, and this world.

In shaa Allah (God Willing) this will be marked down as a good deed for me and all those who have benefited from this book and passed it along. I began this project to better myself and I hope it pays off.

"If you don't help yourself now, you won't be able to help anyone else in the future."— Steve Sanders from his book *Training Camp for Life*.

When I was a young boy, my mother taught me a very simple saying: "Want for your brother, what you want for yourself."

I want to be healthy, wealthy, and a benefit to society. I also want that for my brothers. *In shaa Allah*, together we can make it happen.

Assalamu Alaikum Wa Rahmatullahi Wa Barrakatuh (Peace be unto you and so may the mercy of Allah and His blessings).

MY TRANSITION IN SEVEN STEPS
The Seven-Step Transition

WORKBOOK

Step One: Officially Retire
Step Two: Take a Break
Step Three: Create a Transition Plan and Schedule
Step Four: Get a Mentor
Step Five: Evaluate Your Overall Health
Step Six: Control Your Circle
Step Seven: Write a Goodbye Letter

STEP ONE: OFFICIALLY RETIRE

Announce it, write it, and believe it. You're done. Your playing days are over. Come to grips with it and embrace it. The sooner you get out of your own way, the better. This will not be a simple declaration. We've spent our entire career proving people wrong. And now we feel as though this is our biggest challenge. I'm here to let you know, it's over. You've accomplished something very few in the world have. Look at your accomplishments. Remember where it all started. That young kid with a dream. Those frequent conversations with doubters and even yourself. Those conversations that ended with, "just watch." We've all had them, and today we can sit back and say, "I did it." How many individuals would kill for the opportunities you've had? How many young people look at you with amazement because of your accomplishments? Ask any young prospect if they would trade places with you, and you'll hear a resounding YES!

You are a success.

You are loved. So often we focus on the wrong things, let us focus on the right ones. It's easy to see the blessings of others and feel as though we are insufficient, or not as blessed. It's harder to see the struggles of others and the obstacles they have overcome to reach their heights. It's easy to see our own struggles, but tougher to notice our blessings.

The odds of a high school football player making it to the NFL are 0.08%. Those aren't fantastic odds, but you did it. Over our career we were shunned for patting ourselves on the back. Now is the time, where we can safely and comfortably applaud ourselves. We've accomplished something that others merely dream about.

Standing ovation to the individuals who set out to accomplish their dreams and did it.

STEP TWO: TAKE A BREAK

A real break. Get away from it all and unplug. Go somewhere where no one knows or really cares about football. Go somewhere where you can assimilate into the culture and let your hair down. This is a real vacation. A vacation of the mind, body, and soul. Turn your cell phone off, don't check your email, and don't think about football. We've always had vacations that were short and not as enjoyable, because we didn't want to disturb our training schedule.

You've worked hard, now it's time to play hard. Spare no expense, and treat yourself. First class accommodations throughout the entire trip. Sit back and relax. Call ahead and tell your destination you are coming for a peaceful stay. Have the staff remove the alarm clocks, or unplug them. Sleep in. Eat junk food. Go for a walk. Buy a good book. Read outside. Do things you were never able to because of always being on call. Enjoy your freedom.

For the first time in your life, you have to be totally selfish. You've taken care of everyone else's needs, but have ignored your own. You were always the one that had to be strong and bear the burdens of others. Those shoulders get tired after carrying all of those people, neighborhoods, organizations and cities. We've been lifting upper body our whole career, and forgot about our own legs.

Now it's time to kick those feet up. Our leg workout now consists of us walking away from the clutter and confusion, towards the calm and peace. This trip is much needed and much deserved.

Congratulations on a great career.

When you get back from your trip, you can think about your next step, but for now, enjoy.

STEP THREE: CREATE A TRANSITION PLAN AND CORRESPONDING SCHEDULE

Controlled vs. Chaotic.

Our lives were very controlled and punctual, and now it may seem as though we're in a free-for-all. We're coming from an institution that passed out itineraries on a daily basis. We knew what we were supposed to do and when, down to the minute.

Take the same approach in your transition.

My schedule consists of my to-do lists and the steps to accomplish them. I begin every morning with family time, then personal time, business time, and back to family. This is really about your own personal preferences and what exactly you'd like to get accomplished.

While writing my book, I found the best time for me to write was after everyone went to sleep. Find your best time to accomplish your daily tasks and goals, then write them out.

Create your daily itinerary to success.

STEP FOUR: GET A MENTOR

You need someone with knowledge and experience to be your new Head Coach. They will instruct you on the game plan of retirement, while being sympathetic to your delicate psyche. Good mentors have a few characteristics in common. The most important characteristic is that they care about your well-being. They care that you succeed because when you succeed, they feel an internal happiness. Make sure the individual you enlist cares. The individual should "want for his brother, what he wants for himself."

The second characteristic is that they are knowledgeable in the field. A mentor has to be able to understand your situation and know pertinent information that will aid you in being successful.

The third characteristic is to be a foreseer. The mentor must be able to accurately anticipate future events that you will encounter, and provide you with tools to address those situations.

The fourth characteristic is to be positive. Your mentor must always be an optimist rather than a pessimist. The last thing we need in our time of grief and sorrow is someone else unloading their problems on us. You know those individuals. The ones who are constantly complaining about what they don't have and what someone else has. These are not the individuals you want leading your life. A mentor must have key qualities of leadership and a résumé of success.

The final characteristic of a good mentor, is that the mentor must be reachable. You will depend on this mentor and need him at all hours of the day. Different situations will arise that are new experiences for you. A veteran mentor can assist you through these challenges.

My mentor made sure I understood what retirement benefits I was entitled to, as well as realistic short term goals that would keep me on a positive track.

When I received the return letter after being denied my LOD, I was enraged and thought about a Twitter Tirade II. I took a deep breath and phoned my mentor. He informed me that many guys are denied on their first application.

The NFL is a business. A big BIG business. The only thing that matters is the bottom line. The profit line. The NFL is and will continue to be a profitable business.

I benefited from it, as did my cohorts. We don't wish the NFL was unprofitable, we just don't understand the treatment of the players who make it all possible.

The players play the game, and without the players there will be no game. I hope this changes in the future, but in the meantime, the players must stick together and educate those that come after us on the mindset of the NFL. My mentor educated me on the views of the NFL, and how I must adopt similar views when dealing with them. The NFL views itself and all of its relationships as a business relationship.

I must do the same. We must do the same. I played for the Denver Broncos, and loved every minute of it. Like every player before me, and everyone after me, there would be a time that I would no longer be a Denver Bronco.

I can't take it personally, because it's just business. I'm thankful for my mentor and his sound advice.

STEP FIVE: EVALUATE YOUR OVERALL HEALTH

P hysically, mentally, and emotionally, you are different.

With every transition, we are leaving one situation and one set of circumstances to go to another situation with different circumstances. A small piece of us stays behind, and we have to adjust. We owe it to ourselves to have an honest interpretation of our health. I recommend getting professional help for every evaluation. An Internal Medicine Specialist as well as a Psychiatrist.

As tough as the physical transition is, it's nothing compared to the mental transition. We loved what we did, and we have spent an extensive portion of our lives establishing ourselves on this plateau. When we lose something that we love, it's human nature to go through grief. The grieving process takes on many faces, but a familiar face is that of depression. Transition leads to depression, and depression leads to despair. If we are not careful, this moment of despair can lead to an overwhelming cycle of despondency. It's easy to focus on the things we've lost and justify our downtrodden feelings, but it's tougher to see what we've gained in our transition.
I myself can look at money, relationships, homes, and of course my playing career, as things I've lost. The pessimistic portion of my brain wants me to focus on these things and dig myself deeper and deeper.

God willing, I will not let it. I will get the proper help and I pray you do the same as well.

STEP SIX: CONTROL YOUR CIRCLE

Your circle consist of those determining factors in your life that you can control. Much of our time during a transition is occupied by things we can not control. I can control going to a doctor visit for an evaluation of my disability benefits, but I can not control what that doctor will write and send to the NFL. I can control how I spend my money, but I can not control how my parents spend their money. I can control and limit my interactions on social media, but I can not control the responses I will receive. Although I may think of these things I can not control, I shouldn't exhaust much energy towards these stressors. The main elements of your circle include your Family, your Identity, your Finances and your Attitude.

FIFA.

Think soccer, when you think of your circle. A soccer ball, or fútbol, is round. Your circle is round, and in that soccer ball are your keys to success. The things you truly care about, and those things you truly control, are in that soccer ball. Let's do an exercise right now.
I want you to go to a private place, where you're not bothered, there are no sounds, and it's just you and these pages. Sit down, lie down, or do whatever you can to get comfortable. Now I want you to close your eyes, take a deep breath, focus on being present, and clear your mind. Now I have your attention, your mind is clear, and we can begin our exercise.

Imagine you reside in Los Angeles, California, United States of America.

It's 8:30 P.M. Pacific Standard Time. There isn't a cloud in the sky, because it's California. It's 70 degrees. You're driving your car, and you pull over to the side of the road. You get out of your vehicle to witness the beauty of the night. You look up in the sky and see a million bright stars accompanied by a full moon.

You're at peace.

You're all by yourself with no other vehicles or pedestrians around. It's just you and nature. All of a sudden, the ground begins to shake. Not just a "someone's trying to wake you up" shake, but an "OH MY GOD! OH MY GOD! OH MY GOD!" shake. You're at the epicenter of a magnitude 6.0 Earthquake. The ground is swaying beneath your feet, trees are falling, and your vehicle begins to slide down the hill. You run after your vehicle, jump in and speed off...

Where are you headed?

You pick up your cellphone...Who do you call?

What are your first instincts?

The answer to those questions, are inside of your soccer ball. Were you worried about getting that promotion at work? Were you worried about how many followers you had on social media? Were you worried about anything that you began this exercise worried about?

Probably not.

You were worried about the immediate well-being of yourself and your family. You cared about your FIFA. Visualization is a powerful tool. It has helped many professional athletes achieve heights that previously were only dreamt of. I was first introduced to visualization by my football coach, my junior year in college. He would turn down the lights at the end of every meeting, and tell us to envision making plays, playing well, and enjoying the moment with my teammates. I use visualization now, because I know it works. I plan to no longer worry or stress about those things I can not control and focus on what I can control.

I care about my Family, Identity, Finances and Attitude.

The four things I can control.

Family-IFA

We begin with our family. My wife and three children are within my control. I can't control them physically, but I can control how I act and interact with them. I can control how I treat them and how I carry myself around them. I have been entrusted to care, provide and protect them.

F-Identity-FA

Secondly is our Identity. Who we are. I identify myself as a Husband, Father, Son, Brother, Author, and Muslim. To be better at all of these, I have come up with three small goals that if done consistently, will make me better at my respective titles. An example is that of a Husband. For me to be a better Husband, I write down three objectives. One-woman man, Service, and Sharpen the saw.

Number one is to be a ONE woman man. I must treat my wife like the queen she is and give her the attention, energy, and time she deserves.

Number two is I must serve my wife. This doesn't necessarily mean serve her like a butler, though sometimes the situation may call for this. This serving of my wife is to serve her as I would want her to serve me, and how she has served me since we have been married. Love is reciprocal. Service to a loved one is one of the highest forms of joy a person can experience. She has been there for me through surgeries, and other ailments, where she would wait on me hand and foot. Now is a good time for me to return the favor. To serve my wife is to make her life easier. If changing a diaper, picking up the children from school, or cooking dinner means a moment of relaxation for my wife, then I will do it.

Number three on the list, is to sharpen the saw. When I first began to court my wife, I would do anything to make her smile and feel comfortable. I would send her funny messages throughout the day, and do whatever else would put a smile on her face.

As the years went by, I forgot how important that was to our relationship. I have taken her for granted, and used my profession, our children and things outside of my control as excuses for not performing my husbandly duties. I can control these small steps to becoming a better husband, and I will take care of them.

FI-Finances-A

After our Family and Identity sits our Finances.

Frivolous Finances Fail Families.

Take control of your finances, or the worrying of the lack of finances, will take control over you. First off, do not let anyone "Loan," "Borrow," or "Hold" any money. In every Defensive Back room across the NFL, there are four letters etched in stone.

Those four letters are G-T-F-B.

When you retire, regardless of your position, you must become a DB and use these four letters. These four letters not only save touchdowns, but they save marriages. The Next time someone asks you for money, simply reply G-T-F-B.

Get The ~~Fuck~~ Back!

If you weren't there, who would they call, email, or text? Let them go to a bank and apply for a personal loan. We think by giving people money we're doing a good deed, but we're not. We're enablers to addicts. These people are addicted to leeching off of others. They are using us to get what they want, then when the well dries up, they will move right along and not even send a "get well soon" card.

You need not look far for these individuals, they're usually the ones wearing your jersey every time they leave the house. They want everyone to know that they're on the payroll, and the onlookers are not.

We all want to buy our mother a mansion and an expensive car. A house with the utility bills and groceries forever taken care of. For many of us as professional athletes, this will never happen. We won't see the tens or hundreds of millions of dollars that are now synonymous with the facade of being a professional athlete. Which in my opinion, is a good thing. When one has tremendous wealth, but no financial knowledge or financial literacy, it can be a detriment to their longevity of maintaining such wealth. Just as we have a salary cap in sports, there needs to be a salary cap for the "Taking Care" of ones extended family. We must learn to say "No." The power of the word No, is unmistakable. When I go to a car dealership, my biggest power play is saying "No" and walking away. The car salesman doesn't want that, and therefore will do everything in his power to prevent me from saying no.

As we begin our career and earning this higher level of salary, many people will come around to get what they feel is owed to them. Parents, siblings, cousins, friends, long lost relatives, and neighbors will be right by your side. As Hip Hop icon Snoop Dogg said in his 1996 Hit Single *Gin and Juice*, "Everybody got they cups, but they ain't chipped in."

Did your parents help you? Yes.

Did your siblings? Yes.

Did your coach? Yes.

Do you owe them anything outside of a "Thank You?"

No.

Your parents and loved ones should understand this if they truly love you. If they were helping you achieve your dream, for the sake of God and for the sake of you accomplishing your dreams, then their payment is in you accomplishing that dream. Not in the form of a cash payment.

Sometimes we as focal points in our families, feel obligated to bear the weight of the world on our shoulders. The truth is, we can't carry such a load. To make sure we are not lifting more than the maximum capacity allowed on our shoulders, we will implement the *Sibling Salary Cap*.

The *Sibling Salary Cap* is a hard cap, meaning it cannot be altered. The rules are set, and there are steep consequences for not abiding by these rules. We will break it down into three levels.

Parents, Siblings, and Other.

Your entourage, or those individuals who think they're in your entourage, fit into the "Other" category. Keep this in mind when you are choosing the individuals you surround yourself with. They should elevate you in faith or wealth by their association. If this is not the case, cut them loose because sooner or later they will weigh you down, and you'll eventually sink. For our *Sibling Salary Cap* we will begin on the ground floor, or Level 1.

Level one is Level Other: For those individuals who you would like to do something nice for, and would like to show them your gratitude, you will give them a signed photo and a hand written letter. In the letter you will focus on thanking them for all their contributions, and how appreciative you are to have them in your corner. That's it. No gold chains, cars, condos, stipends, or bail money. Next up, is Level 2.

Level two is Level Siblings: For your dearest companions, who fought with you day and night, who held you accountable, who believed in you, maybe even took care of you when your parents weren't able to, who reaffirmed your goals and dreams, you want to thank them properly. They also receive a signed photo and hand written letter, but they also receive a gift of your choosing. This gift should be a one-time gift, and relative to your affordability. I myself have eleven brothers and sisters, six half brothers and sisters, and four step brothers and sisters.

Giving my siblings twenty one personal gifts is a bit tough—especially not having grown up with most of them—but I still tried to thank them for being there for me. These are not "break the bank" gifts, they're more thoughtful or helpful gifts. When Esa graduated from High School and prepared to go to WSU, I saw it as an opportunity to give him a Level two gift. My gift to him was paying for his admission to his Grad Night Party and his plane ticket to college.

That was it.

He was thankful, and I felt good about helping him. I didn't get him a debit card attached to my bank account and allow him the financial flexibility to run amok at the shopping malls. Now we move to the last level of our *Sibling Salary Cap*. This is the penthouse, where all of the emotions like guilt and feelings of being indebted appear. This is the toughest level. I have never talked back to my parents, and have definitely never told them no, so it was exponentially tough to tell them "No" in this instance. But if you don't tell them no, you're on the fast track to going broke. This is Level 3.

Level three is Level Parents: Your parents brought you into this world, and they can "take you out," as many claim. The fact remains however, that you did not ask to be brought into this world. You were not conceived and nurtured for the sole purpose of retiring your parents at a young age. You were nurtured and groomed because that is what parents do. That is what their job description requires. Parents are to take care of their children. I am not advocating for the abandonment of love or assistance to one's parents. I am however advocating for the change in the mindset and requirements of this assistance. I can love my parents without buying them a thing. They surely have loved me without purchases in the past, so why must it be a double standard now?

I love to give gifts.

I am an individual who wants to make sure these gifts are given purely to put a smile on the recipient's face and to show how grateful I am to have that person in my life.

Your parents will receive the perks from Level's 1 & 2, but will also receive a substantial gift. This substantial gift is a one-time gift, and it should not cause undue stress or pressure on the receiver of this gift. Many athletes want to buy their parents a home or at least rent them a nicer home. This is fine, as long as the upkeep of this home can be taken care of by your parents. If you buy your parents a million dollar home with a $5,000 a month upkeep—but your parents make $3,000 a month—this won't work. If you would like to rent them a bigger home, then maybe set aside some money that is strictly for your parents rent, put it in an account, and distribute it to them monthly.

There is no replenishment of this account. Inform your parents that once this money is gone, it's gone forever. Again, do not force your parents to live above their means, or quietly they will resent you for it. The gift should be a one-time thing, then it's done.

For example, if instead of a home you'd like to buy them a nice car instead for them to share (if they are married), this should also be a one-time payment. If you can't buy it cash, don't buy it. There are plenty of affordable nice cars that are new or nearly new. Do your research and talk with your parents about what they would like. Make sure your parents can handle the upkeep of this car. Insurance, gas, and maintenance costs should all be handled by your parents. Not you. Inform your parents of your *Sibling Salary Cap*, and let them know it's a one-time thing. Be upfront, this way there is no confusion.

Some parents may simply prefer cash over a gift. That's okay too. Just make sure they know, this is not a sitcom. There will be no syndicated episodes rerunning thereafter. This sum should be modest. Cash can make people go crazy. Don't send your parents to the loony bin.

After the giving of gifts and the writing of letters are complete, you are free. You no longer have to get in an argument with your spouse over paying for this person's or that person's situation. It's done.

The *Sibling Salary Cap* is simple, and when used properly it can prevent major breakdowns later on. To sum up the *Sibling Salary Cap*, we have three levels: Level Parents, Level Siblings and Level Other. All levels receive a signed photo and handwritten thank you letter. Level Parents and Level Siblings receive a thoughtful gift, with Level Parents also receiving a substantial gift. These are one time things because your focus needs to be on taking care of your FIFA. Your extended family are not on full scholarship for the rest of their lives. Another important aspect of our finances is our charitable contributions.

In the Christian Church, their members pay 10 percent of their annual income to the Church in the form of tithes. In Islam we, pay 2.5 percent of our wealth, termed *Zakah* or *Zakat*, annually to the poor or those in need. These are the bare minimums for charitable giving.

Something I believe will be especially purposeful for us as professional athletes is helping those individuals who we used to be. This can be in the form of buying cleats or jerseys for your old Pop Warner team, donating to your high school athletics program, or donating to your local community center or Boys and Girls Club.

Another donation you can make is a donation of your time. Youth tend to remember the times you spent with them more than how much you spent on them. The recipients of these donations will truly appreciate it, and you will be able to see your gift in motion.

FIF-Attitude

I first thought the word attitude referred to a tantrum thrown by a teenage girl. "She has an attitude," was the only way I referenced the idea of having an attitude. That changed with the same coach who taught me the importance of visualization. Coach Kenneth Edward Greene or "KG the Kid," as he was known in the Defensive Back room at Washington State University, first introduced me to what Attitude really meant. Coach Greene, shortly after introducing himself, handed every DB in the room a piece of paper with the word ATTITUDE inscribed on the top of the page. There were a few raised eyebrows in the room, some giggles, and of course some resentment. He was a new coach in a room as talented as any room in the country.

Eight of the 12 DB's in the room went on to the NFL. My two closest friends were the leaders of the room, they were both All American and All Pac-10 Conference performers. I knew that if they ripped up the paper and threw it over their shoulders, the group would follow suit. Instead, they put their heads down and began to read. We all began to read. This was my first introduction to self-motivation and psychotherapy. I took a deep breath, looked down, and began to read...

ATTITUDE

"The longer I live, the more I realize the impact of attitude on life. Attitude, to me is more important than facts. It is more important than the past, than education, than money, than circumstances, than failures, than successes, than what other people think or say or do. It is more important than appearance, giftedness or skill. It will make or break a company...a church...a home. The remarkable thing is we have a choice every day regarding the attitude we will embrace for that day. We cannot change our past. We cannot change the fact that people will act in a certain way. We cannot change the inevitable. The only thing we can do is play on the one string we have, and that is our attitude. I am convinced that life is 10% what happens to me and 90% how I react to it. And so it is with you. We are in charge of our attitudes."—Charles Swindoll

As I finished reading, I stared at the page in a state of awe. It was the most powerful, non-religious material, I had ever read. I looked up to measure the temperament of the room. I wondered if this simple poem struck a chord in the other DBs, like it did with me. I remember KG the Kid asking for feedback, and our leader, my roommate, Erik spoke up. He was a fearless, soft spoken young man. He began his illustrious response by saying, "Thank You." He, like all of us didn't know what to expect with a new coach handing out pieces of paper. After the thank you, he touched briefly on his upbringing and home life, then broke into a candid account of his goals and fears of not achieving those goals. He admitted this poem reassured him of himself and his mission. His life was truly in his own hands. I nodded my head in agreement and wondered how this small poem on a single sheet of paper could be so heavy.

We committed the poem to memory and would recite it periodically throughout the season. We had a great season, finishing with 10 wins and three losses, with the DB's leading the way for the team. It was a memorable ride, and we can trace the roots of our success to changing our attitude. I challenge you to commit to playing on the one string that you have, and that is your attitude. I challenge you, and myself, to undertake a positive attitude every day. With that, we conclude our circle. We are in charge of our circle.

Our Family, Our Identity, Our Finances and Our Attitude.

Those familiar with Stephen Covey's transcendent book *The 7 Habits of Highly Effective People*, recognize some of the familiar terms of our circle, like "sharpen the saw" and "service."

In his *7 Habits* book, Dr. Covey has the reader do a simple exercise. This exercise, literally changed my outlook on my life. I would like you to partake in this written exercise as well. Begin by writing down all of your worries, stresses, and points of concern.

My list included my parents, my siblings, my marriage, raising my children, my income, my money, my disability benefits, women, my religious involvement, my health, my physique, my appearance, my mood, my book, the NFL, and a possible relocation.
After writing the list down, I had to take a step back to analyze and reflect on all of my worries. Until putting pen to the pad, I had no idea all of these factors were weighing on my mind. After writing your list, draw a circle. In that circle, place those worries that you can control. My list got dramatically smaller.

The only thing in my circle was my marriage, raising my children, my money, my religious involvement, my health, my physique, my appearance, my mood, and my book. All those things not in my circle were discarded from the worrying portion of the brain. I couldn't control them, therefore, they need not occupy my mental space.

Discarding my parents and siblings from the worrisome part of my brain did not mean discarding them from my life. It meant that I could not control them, only my interaction with them. Therefore, I need not lie awake at night wondering if my parents were going to do whatever it was that I wanted them to do. They're their own people, and they will do what they want to do. There is no need stressing over those decisions. I felt a sizable weight lifted off my shoulders. I was able to breathe and sleep easier. I'm thankful for Dr. Covey's insight, and I hope this exercise proved as useful to you as it has been for me.

Control your circle. Family-Identity-Finances-Attitude.

STEP SEVEN: WRITE A GOODBYE LETTER

During one of my weekly marriage counseling sessions, my wife and I sat on a leather love seat at opposite ends. As my wife began to delve into the topics of discussion, the counselor keyed in on me. She told me I loved my wife, but I also loved football. Because I had lost football, I was grieving and would continue to grieve until I let it go. She recommended I write a Goodbye Letter to the NFL that served as my final detachment from the League I once loved.

After this letter, I was not allowed to let it control me, blame it for not loving me back, or worry about it. My mood changed dramatically on the couch, and I was able to understand what had been dragging me down.

I had not given the NFL a proper goodbye, and it was interfering with my ability to love and show love to my loved ones. This goodbye letter is not a eulogy, but it is eerily similar. We are laying to rest our emotional attachment and need of the NFL. This letter should be taken seriously and be well thought out.

Take some time thinking about what you would like to say, and the best way to say it. Be honest, be open, and be content. Understand where you are now, the person you have become, and the fact that you would not be this person had it not been for your past.

This is our final step to a successful Transition, God willing.

TRANSITION ACTIVITIES

SEVEN STEPS

1..

2..

3..

4..

5..

6..

7..

Step 1 Activities

RETIRE

1. Write a short formal retirement statement for whatever you are Transitioning from.
2. In your statement include the highlights of your experience and be gracious and grateful.
3. Close the door on a possible return. Your retirement is final. Write this in your statement.
4. Disclose this retirement to those closest to you before making it public knowledge.
5. Post your retirement statement online.

NOTES

....

....

....

....

....

....

....

....

Step 2 Activities

TAKE A BREAK

1. Identify three destinations that remind you of peace, tranquility and serenity.
2. This destination should not be associated with what you are transitioning from. It should not remind you of what you left, but of what you are heading towards. Of the three destinations, remove any destination that will remind you of your past.
3. Plan a three to five day vacation. Vacate your attachments. Vacate your worries.
4. Pick one of the three destinations and book the trip.
5. GO!

NOTES

....

....

....

....

....

....

....

Step 3 Activities

MAKE A TRANSITION PLAN AND SCHEDULE

1. Identify three goals you would like to accomplish and write them down.
2. Underneath each goal write three plans that will help you achieve these goals.
3. Underneath each plan write three steps that if done consistently, will help you achieve the plan that will help you accomplish your goal.
4. Write out a monthly calendar, weekly organizer and daily planner. The goal is to have small accomplishments daily that contribute to you accomplishing bigger tasks weekly which directly relate to accomplishing major milestones monthly.
5. Post your schedule where you can see it daily.

NOTES

....

....

....

....

....

....

Step 4 Activities

GET A MENTOR

1. Identify five individuals who you think would be good mentors.
2. Tell the prospective mentors you need help and pay attention to the one who feels it is their duty to take you by the hand and lead you to safety.
3. Write down three tasks from your mentor and message them at the completion of each task.
4. Schedule a time to speak with your mentor weekly. Take notes and ask three specific questions for your mentor that directly relate to your Transition.
5. Put your mentor on your favorites list in your phone.

NOTES

....

....

....

....

....

....

....

Step 5 Activities

YOUR OVERALL HEALTH

1. Make a list of healthcare professionals in your area. Identify three professionals that will assist in your evaluation and subsequent healing. Schedule appointments for all three professionals.
2. Before you walk into the office, write down how you feel. After you leave the office, write down how you feel.
3. Relax, be honest and forthcoming with these professionals. They are there to help you. If you feel as though your well-being is not their top priority, find another professional.
4. Write down your sleep pattern, how much and what you're eating as well as how much you are exercising. Write down a specific fun activity, a time where you can sit and relax, as well as an event you can plan. This list should be easily accessible.
5. Start a health journal that you write in and update daily.

NOTES

....

....

....

....

Step 6 Activities

CONTROL YOUR CIRCLE

1. Write down the members of your family that are your dependents. They are the only ones allowed in the first "F" section of your circle.
2. Write down three steps to improve your Identity and read the ATTITUDE poem daily.
3. When you looked in the mirror this morning, did you like what you saw? Why or why not? What can you do to make it better? Write three things you will do today that will improve how you feel tomorrow.
4. Write out your *Sibling Salary Cap* and complete it. Create a monthly balance sheet of all income and expenses. Post it where you can see it.
5. Write a list of everything that worries you, stresses you out or occupies your mind. Draw a circle and include the things on the list that you can control. Write the remaining things on the list outside of the circle. Focus on the items inside the circle.

NOTES

....

....

....

....

Step 7 Activities

WRITE A GOODBYE LETTER

1. Write your letter.
2. Do not rush this letter. The timing of it is not as important as writing a thoughtful piece.
3. Identify specific times, dates, or occasions that will give the letter true substance.
4. Properly address the letter to whom represents what you are Transitioning from.
5. Handwrite and mail the letter.

NOTES

....

....

....

....

....

....

....

GOODBYE

July 4th, 2014
National Football League
345 Park Ave
New York, NY 10154 United States

Dear NFL,

Peace and blessings. I pray this letter reaches you in the highest levels of success, viewership, and Employee and Customer satisfaction. I am writing you today to tell you Goodbye. For seven illustrious years, I was fortunate to call myself an Active NFL Player. I know the average career lasts only three and a half years, so I feel extremely grateful that you allowed me to be above average. You were an intimidating force and you always did what was best for you, regardless of who you hurt in the process. I felt hurt at times, but now I see you were just doing what you had to do. I thank you for being honest with me and making me earn everything I attained.

I loved you with all of my heart, and I thank you for loving me back. It was tough love, but at times, that's the best love for us. You made me earn your respect, the respect of my peers, and my own self-respect. I've always been a quiet person, but you forced me to break out of my shell. You showed me how to be a man. I left my parents' house at the age of 16, and never fully learned how to be a man until I stepped foot in your Locker Room. You taught me what it meant to sacrifice, to lead, to be counted on, and to be tough. You kept telling me that if I worked hard enough, I would accomplish my aspirations, goals and dreams. You taught me the early bird doesn't get the worm unless the early bird prepares properly. You taught me practice doesn't make perfect, it makes permanent. Perfect practice makes perfect. You taught me not to judge a book by its cover because that book will knock you on your rear end, regardless of size. The lessons you taught me are too many to count, but I want you to know, I truly appreciate them.

From the very first time I laid eyes on you, I knew I wanted in. My first memory of the NFL was at the ripe age of two years old. One of my aunts returned to Los Angeles, California from a Midwest trip to Chicago, Illinois. She came bearing gifts and bestowed on me a Chicago Bears Jersey. The Bears were fresh off a win in Super Bowl XX. I didn't know what football or a Super Bowl was, but I was hooked. I wore that jersey nearly every day until the age of five. I'm quite sure it looked more like a bib than a jersey at that point, but I loved it. I loved you. I loved the idea of running, throwing, jumping and catching an oval shaped ball. It would be many years until I was able to play organized football, but none the less, I knew I wanted to dance with you when I got older.

As I grew older my love for you became stronger and stronger. I'm not afraid to admit you were my first real crush. I loved you more than I loved my 3rd grade teacher. I remember when my dad took me to see my first game at the Los Angeles Coliseum. The game featured the hometown Los Angeles Raiders versus the Washington Redskins. I'm not sure what year, or how old I was, but I don't remember sitting down. There weren't many people at the game, so we were able to get seats so close, I could see the names on the back of the players jerseys. I fantasized about one day the back of a jersey reading "ABDULLAH," with me in it. I knew it was just a dream, but aren't kids supposed to dream? The Raiders won the game 37-24 to cap a perfect first date between us. Unfortunately like most crushes, they soon crash and burn. You broke my heart by moving my LA Raiders to Oakland, without even saying goodbye. How could you do this to me? I loved you! We were perfect for each other. Sure I didn't have a job, and couldn't afford tickets, but I loved you. Isn't love enough? Isn't love supposed to trump all including money? I cried a lot, because I knew you had moved on, but I was still holding on in hopes that you would change your mind and come back where you belonged. You belonged with me. I was young and naive to think that way, but I'm glad you left. You made me appreciate the time we had together. You showed me that if I grew up, got my teeth fixed, gained more muscles and got taller, one day you may come back to me. I believed in us, and I believed it wasn't just lust, but love. I vowed the next time you saw me, you would wonder what happened to the kid with the unkempt afro and coke bottle glasses. I would be unrecognizable, and you would fall head over heels in love with me.

I placed posters on my wall of the players you were dating like Jerry Rice and Ronnie Lott. I looked at them and wondered how you chose them over me. I mean sure they were bigger, stronger, faster, more good looking, more athletic, and older than me, but they didn't love you like I did. I used these posters as motivation as I began to workout in my room. Every day when I woke up, and every night before I went to bed, I did 100 pushups.

I knew you liked your men strong, so I wanted to be extra strong just for you. I also knew you liked your men tall, so I started taking naps. My best friend Embert told me, if I took more naps, I would grow. My days consisted of prayer, pushups, eating, napping, and playing. I sacrificed time outside with my friends, to make sure I slept as much as possible. Love is about sacrifice, and I loved you. You were gone, but you had not been forgotten. As my body began to change, and my legs began to stretch out, my stepfather took it upon himself to help me prepare for the day I met you again. He signed me up to play Pop Warner Football in a suburb of Los Angeles.

The Chino Pop Warner Broncos were the first step in my football life. I had never put on football pads or a helmet, so as you can imagine, I didn't know what to expect. The first time I lined up to do a football drill, I said a prayer and thought of you. I had to make a good impression on you, even though you weren't watching. I knew that if this impression was good enough, you would hear about it. I laid on my back for what seemed like an eternity. Another player five yards away, on his back. I was to wait for the blowing of the whistle, then jump up and dive head first into my opponent's chest. When the whistle blew, I hopped up like a cat searching for mice. I beat my combatant to his feet, and had the edge in velocity, speed and power. I closed my eyes, as I imagined kissing you for the first time, and pounced on my prey. The poor young lad didn't stand a chance. I opened my eyes to the entire team surrounding me and lifting me up as though I were a victorious Roman gladiator. My Head Coach, Coach Parhms, announced to the onlookers that one day, you and I would be holding hands and I would be courting you. I passed the first test you sent my way and anxiously anticipated the next one.

I was homeschooled throughout my childhood, and knew if I were to be ready to meet you again, I would have to go back and play football at a public high school. My mother reluctantly enrolled me at Pomona High School in Pomona, California, but it came with a compromise. I was able to attend high school, but I would start two years ahead of my age group. I was a 14 year old sophomore. To make matters worse, my mother enrolled me after football season, so I would have to wait until my junior year to play. I was frustrated, but I had my eyes on you, and would do anything to gain your approval. When my junior year came, I was a five foot nine inch tall, 145 pound, 15 year old with bad eyesight. After a few practices the coaches determined that I would need to play Junior Varsity and earn my way on to the Varsity football team. I played well and had an opportunity to play on the Varsity team after the second game of the season. I was a fish out of water on Varsity. I wore Number 60, yes 6-0, and a Thurman Thomas face mask on my helmet. I'm still convinced that I am the only defensive back in the history of football to wear the number 60. Sixty is a number reserved for slow guys, and I apparently was one of them.

The game was too fast for me, and I couldn't see a thing. The bar right down the middle of my face mask made it hard to focus on anything, other than the bar right in front of my face. Couple that with the fact I had 20/100 vision, and you have a disaster. On the opening kickoff of the one and only varsity game I played my junior year, I ran right by the guy with the ball, because I couldn't see he had the ball in his hands. On Junior Varsity we played during the daytime, but on Varsity we played at night. I could manage in the day, but at night was a different story. I needed glasses, goggles, or contacts, but that was out of reach for my parents. I made a promise to myself and to you, that I wouldn't let the excuse of having bad eyesight be a reason I wouldn't see you again. During the summer before my senior year in High School, I got a job working at the Pomona Water Department, with the sole intention of buying contacts to play football. I was very fortunate to earn enough to go to the optometrist, then get a prescription and a seasons' worth of contacts. Now that I could see, I wreaked havoc on high school houseboys. I was rewarded with a full scholarship offer to Washington State University. Go Cougs!

I kept climbing the ladder, envisioning the day that you would one day crown me your prince. I made it through Pop Warner and High School, but now it was the final test. Division 1A Football.

When I stepped on campus at WSU, I quickly learned that I was not the only one preparing to show up at your father's door to ask for your hand. I was now an even six feet tall and weighed 175 pounds. I began to take protein, lift weights, and workout at an unbelievable pace. I wanted my chest to stick out, so I made sure I aligned myself with other guys who I thought were also preparing to meet you. Upon my arrival at campus, my friend and teammate Jason David made a bold declaration. He vowed that the four freshmen defensive backs—recruited in the year 2000 to WSU— would all go to the League. At the time, Hip Hop Hustler and Mogul Jay-Z, released a CD with his Roc-A-Fella crew entitled *The Dynasty*. JD coined the four freshmen DB's, The Dynasty. The Dynasty consisted of Jason David, Erik Coleman, Karl Paymah and me. As my favorite rapper once said, "Ain't no fun, if the homies can't have none." I was willing to share you with my three brothers from another mother, but no one else. My brothers pushed me to be great, and even after I tore my Anterior Cruciate Ligament in my sophomore year, they still believed in me that I would be healthy enough to dance with you some day. They were right.

On April 24th, 2005, you asked me to go steady. You noticed me noticing you while you pretended not to notice me, but I noticed. You welcomed me with open arms and I cried like a baby. The moment I dreamt of was finally here. I would now get to see ABDULLAH on the back of an NFL jersey. Thank you for making my dreams come true. I appreciate you not hanging up on me when I started to cry on the phone. I know you like your men big and strong, but I couldn't help but be overwhelmed with emotions. All the sacrifices, all the hard work, and all the prayers had finally synergized. I still remember walking into my first Locker Room and seeing Tampa Bay Buccaneers-DB-Number 35-Hamza Abdullah. I wasn't sure how I was supposed to react, so I glanced around the room to see what the other players were doing. Of course, they were doing the same thing I was doing. I didn't want to be "That Guy." That guy that did things against the grain, so I just sat down at my locker and pretended like I had been there before. There was only one problem. I hadn't been there before. I hadn't seen how beautiful you were up close. I wanted to take pictures with you, and kiss you all over. I wanted the moment to last forever, but it didn't. My stay in Tampa Bay was short, but you gave me another chance in Denver. Thank you.

From the Chino Pop Warner Broncos to the Denver Broncos. A Hollywood movie script couldn't even make this tale up. I was literally a mile high off the ground. I was swimming in the clouds as you placed me in one of the best football cities in America. People loved you in Denver, more than I had seen anywhere else. Denver Broncos Player Jerseys were considered Formal Attire at Restaurants. It was such an amazing feeling, and for nearly four years you and I were inseparable. We held hands as we walked together though the Rocky Mountains, beaming with beauty. We were the talk of my hometown, Pomona, California and of my college town, Pullman, Washington. Many envied what we had. What we had was special. I didn't want it to end, and for a brief time, it looked like it wouldn't. Then all of a sudden you changed. I saw a side of you that your previous exes warned me about. I learned your business side. I suffered an injury, and you didn't allow me to properly heal, before releasing me. You sent me to the streets to lick my wounds and ponder my next step.

My next step landed me in Cleveland, Ohio playing for the Cleveland Browns. When I made it to Cleveland, I knew you were mad at me and wanted to punish me. You wanted me to grovel and beg to get back with you. I loved you so deeply that I would walk through the darkest valley for you, and that's what Cleveland was. It was painful, depressing, and desolate. At least that's the way it appeared when I arrived. I decided you were trying to teach me a lesson, so I began to see things objectively. The Browns facility was top of the line and resort like. We had valet parking, personal chefs, and childcare. The Muslim community in Cleveland was the most cordial group of people I've ever been around. Brother Jamal and Brother Abdur-Rahman gave me the brothers I was missing. Cleveland wasn't so bad after all. Thank you for teaching me to make the most out of my situation, and to not stereotype or characterize an entire city based on the perception of others. Thank you.

After you broke up with me again in Cleveland, I went to my new home in Seattle, Washington. I desperately wanted to earn your trust again, so I woke up every morning and worked out at the crack of dawn. Rainier Beach High School in Seattle became my second home. I ran, and I ran, but you never noticed me. I checked your website and saw you sign safety after safety, but there was no mention of me. You appeared to move on from me, but you never explained yourself. I was hurt again. This is when I began to understand we had a love/hate relationship. There were times where we loved each other, but there were also times where we hated each other. There were peaks and valleys in our relationship, but at least you were consistent. When you hated me, you really hated me, but when you loved me, you loved me up. After months and months without a call back from you, I began to fathom life without you. I was gearing up to finally pack my things and move on, but you called. You called me while I was on a road trip from Seattle to Los Angeles. You told me you needed me, and you hoped I didn't get ugly or fat. The truth was, I had recently stopped working out on a daily basis, and nearly pulled my hamstring off the bone days earlier, picking up my son's sippy cup. I wasn't in supreme shape, but you gave me the weekend to get ready to see you. I thank you for not rushing me. When I made it to Los Angeles, I immediately went to a local high school and ran more than a distance runner before the Olympics. It obviously paid off, because you gave me another chance. This time with the Arizona Cardinals. I always wanted to play close to home, and now I was only a six hour car ride from home. Thank you.

Arizona is synonymous with retirement, and I'm guessing that's what you were preparing me for. I loved the relaxed family environment of

Chandler, Arizona, a suburb outside of Phoenix. I now had two children and needed to do what was best for them. I felt as though our love candle was beginning to dim, but I tried and tried to add more wax to that candle. I began to use my relationship status with you to earn money off the field and build relationships I would need when the candle finally burned out. I spent nearly three years in Arizona, where I was welcomed into the community and loved like a hometown hero. In Denver you showed me you loved me, but in Arizona you taught me how to love. You introduced me to people that will be life-long friends, as well as the most selfless group of people I had ever met. Brother Ishmael at the Chandler Mosque literally gave me the shirt off his back when he thought I didn't have one. I am thankful that you gave me the opportunity to spend time with people like Brother Ishmael. Without you, we would have never met. Thank you.

I left Arizona and returned to Los Angeles in the hopes of returning to you one day, but that day never came. You have moved on, and now it is time for me to move on. We shared some great times that I will cherish forever. You may not remember me as a player in a year or two, but I hope I left something to remember me as a person by. I loved you with all my heart, but you showed me it isn't the normal love that one sees on the television. This isn't the romantic love we will read about in trashy novels on a layover in Salt Lake City, Utah. It's an operational love. A love that serves you as you serve it. As long as I was in your good graces, you would love and protect me, but once I was gone, I was gone forever. I love what you have done for me and what you have allowed me to do for my family. We may not smile at each other when we pass by, or walk hand in hand, but for a brief period of time, we did. You are more than a memory to me, you are a part of me. From now until forever, people will associate me with you. Thank you for helping me raise my voice, my status, and my ability to help others. I have been blessed with a platform that many people would kill for. Thank you.

Thank you for making me feel special for seven years. Although we had a nasty break up, I can honestly say, I have moved on. I forgive you, and I hope you forgive me. The next time we see each other, I hope you embrace me as you once did. I understand I'll never be an Active Player again, but I have a special request. Please hold on to, and love my brother better than you loved me. When it's his time to move on, please be gentler and more affectionate than you were with me. He's not really big on tough love, or beating around bushes. Be straight with him, and allow him the proper time to build a strong relationship with you. Thank you again, from the bottom of my heart. I pray that we are better because of meeting each other. Farewell, NFL. Peace and be blessed.

Sincerely Yours,

Hamza Abdullah

ACKNOWLEDGMENTS

First, I must thank the One who has allowed this publication to be possible, the Almighty God. It is only by His unlimited grace and mercy that I was able to type a single syllable.

Next, I must thank you the reader. Thank you for bearing with me and taking your time to read my words. If you have stuck around to read this section, I thank you again and sincerely appreciate you spending time with me. I understand that many readers will not be of the Muslim faith, so let me apologize if you felt as though I pushed my religion or way of life upon you, as that was not my intention. I am simply telling my story from my point of view and stating what has helped me on my path of Transition. In Islam, we don't believe in humans having the power or being required to convert others; we endeavor to simply convey the message. I pray that I have presented Islam in a favorable light, and that you felt I did as well.

Special thank you to the NFL Players that allowed me to pen their stories. I pray God blesses you all with better than I could ever repay you for allowing me this great opportunity. I look forward to reading your individual stories in your own books. God willing, I will help where I can. If you trust me, I would love to write it. God willing, this is the beginning of a movement. Thank you for loving for your brother what you've loved for yourself. God bless you, your families, your health, your wealth and your Transitions.

To my lovely wife Alexa, thank you sweetheart, for always being in my corner. It wasn't always easy to deal with me while I was going through my mood swings, bouts of depression, and reckless behavior. I'm thankful you never threw in the towel on me. You continued to fight for me, our relationship, and our children. I am forever indebted to you. You are the definition of a Strong Woman and a Superhero. You are the most selfless person I have ever met, as well as the best person I have ever met. Your brilliance never ceases to amaze me. I feel as though I'm definitely favored by God, because He has sent you to me. You are a Godly woman, and from the first time I met you, I knew it. You weren't Muslim when I met you, but your first question to me was "Do you pray five times a day?" You had very little knowledge of the Islamic religion, but you knew Muslims were supposed to pray five times a day. I responded in the affirmative, and the rest is history. I imagine what would have happened if I were to respond negatively. You most likely would have kicked me to the curb as you did so many other suitors. It has been amazing to watch you grow and gain knowledge despite being a stay at home mom and always pregnant or nursing. During the first eight years of marriage, you were pregnant or nursing every year. That takes stamina, courage, and resolve that most women don't have. You are a mother, wife, chef, teacher, maid, financial advisor, psychiatrist, career counselor, caretaker, chauffeur, hairdresser, personal trainer, personal assistant, accountant, proof reader, and more. You have never complained, nor have you condemned me for my limited assistance. You continue to impress me and I am thankful that God has blessed me with one of His friends to share my life with. I love you with all of my heart, and I pray you forgive me for my many shortcomings and mistakes, and you continue to pray for me and our family. I love you. Come follow me.

To my children Layla, Aqil, Maryam, and Muhammad-YaSeen, thank you for believing in me and treating me like a Superhero. I love you guys so much. Thank you for motivating and inspiring me to be a better Abu, husband, and man. I love you. Thank you.

To my younger brother Husain, look how far we've come. From Pomona to the Publisher. *Allahu Akbar.* Allah is the Greatest. We had a plan and a vision, and we leaned on each other while never letting go of our relationship with Allah. Thank you for being a stand up man and getting on the right track. When you stepped up and manned up, I was forced to do the same. I am thankful that you have always been outspoken and have always had my back. I love you and I pray that now that I am finished with this project, we can finally be neighbors and relax and play video games late into the night like we used to do when we were young. I love you, and I'm proud of you. *Assalamu Alaikum.*

To my older brother Abbas, you're my hero. You sacrificed your dream of being an NBA player so that your two younger brothers could become NFL players. I pray that Allah blesses you with something better. You showed me how to be a man and taught me things that I will forever be thankful for. I'm sorry if you have ever thought I didn't respect you or love you the way you deserved. I've always admired you and wanted to be just like you. I'm proud of you, and it makes me smile every time I see your children. You are a great father, and you have been for longer than you've had kids. You were our father, and for that I am forever in debt to you. You were forced to be a man when you weren't even a teenager yet. We were allowed to make mistakes, but you weren't. You never got the benefit of the doubt, yet you didn't complain. Thank you for not running away. Thank you for taking those whippings for us. You could have left long before you did, but you didn't want to see us cry, so you took them. Thank you.

To my twin sister Hajirah, thank you for telling me to turn my story into a book. Without your words, I would have just written the article, and that would have been the end of my work. You allowed me to tell my story in full, my way. Thank you.

To my younger brother Shaybah, thank you for the phone calls and messages. I didn't answer all the time, but I did receive them. Your messages were always timely and just what I needed to hear. You have always been my spiritual guide, and you have never let me slide too far. Thank you for loving me when I probably didn't deserve it. Thank you.

To my younger sister Aliyyah, thank you for allowing me to be a big brother. You always called me for advice even when you probably had a better option. You trusted me in many of your decisions, and for that I am thankful. I can't wait to help you work with your nonprofit organization so that we can have a positive impact on other children's lives. Thank you.

To my younger brother Esa, thank you for listening. You always called me, not to talk, but to listen. You were a psychology major and you knew that I needed time to vent sometimes, and you allowed me that opportunity. Thank you.

To my younger brother Salih, thank you for your toughness. I get my toughness from you. You remind me so much of me, it's scary. You would run through a wall for me or any of our family members, and I am appreciative of that. When I called you to go to Atlanta, you didn't hesitate. You simply responded, "What time is our flight?" Thank you for being tough when others would be soft.

To my younger brother Mustafa, thank you for having my back online and offline. I saw how you responded to a number of people when I went on my Twitter Tirade. You would have physically fought each one of them if you could. Thank you for having my back. I am blessed to have you as a brother.

To my younger sisters Aisha and Sabriah, and my younger brother Musa, thank you for taking care of our parents while I was going through my Transition. It was tough on me, and you knew it, so you stepped in to help. Thank you for having our parents' back.

To my mother and father, Ummie and Abu Shante, thank you for putting Husain and I in football. We were terrified of football, but you insisted we would like it. You stayed patient with us and allowed us the opportunity to mature as athletes. I know you sacrificed a lot and it wasn't easy raising 12 children. Thank you for putting your children before yourself. To Ummie, thank you for your unwavering support and *duaa*. I always knew when you had made *duaa* for something, even if it was for me to come home. You are close to Allah, and I am thankful you have continued to make *duaa* for me and my overall wellbeing. May Allah have mercy on Abu Shante and accept him into the highest levels of Paradise. I pray that we are reunited in the greatest of gatherings, *Jannatul Firdaus. Assalamu Alaikum.*

To my mother-in-law, Ms. Diane Green; I'm not sure why you allowed me to marry your daughter, but I'm thankful that you did. I definitely out-kicked my coverage marrying Alexa. She has been the rock in my life, and I thank you for raising a special human being. You have spent more time in our home than anyone else, so you've seen this story up close. You have always been there to support me, Alexa, and the children. You read my writings and made me sound smarter than I ever dreamed of. Thank you for encouraging me to read and write more. Maybe one day I can go on *Jeopardy* and win like you.

To Rahsaan, Kenneth, and Tywana Green, thank you for loving me and our family and allowing us to be ourselves. Our trips to Seattle have always been filled with genuine conversation, love, and family time. It was always much needed, and I look forward to our future trip, God willing.

To my Abu, Muhammad Abdullah. Thank you for teaching me to make my Salah (prayers) in the Masjid. You didn't teach me how to catch a ball, ride a bike, or swim, and for a while I resented you for it. However, as I got older, I realized you taught me something of a higher guidance. I pray that God blesses you for instilling this virtue in me. Thank you.

To my older brother Muhammad and my older sister Malika, thank you so much for loving and supporting us. We didn't spend much time together when we were younger, but as we got older we became closer. You guys have called me during my Transition to check on me, and although I didn't answer sometimes, I got your messages and I truly appreciate them. Now that I am done, I pray that we can spend more time together and get the families together. *Assalamu Alaikum.*

To my step brothers and sisters Aaron, Shante, JC, and Sharmenette, thank you for the good times we had when we were younger. I remember having a house full of children and playing all types of games. We may not have had enough food, but we had each other. Thank you for those great memories.

To my cousins the Abdul-Muhaimins, I love all of you. You guys have always been our closest family and have always pushed us to do better. Usama and Huzaifa, I love you so much. When I was a skinny kid with an afro and glasses, you protected me and made sure I could enjoy my High School time without worrying about being picked on. That did a lot for my self-esteem and self-confidence as I grew up into a young man and became able to defend myself. I thank you for nurturing me and showing me the way.

To my best friend Embert Madison, I love you, bro. Every time we see each other or we talk, it's just like the last time we left. It doesn't matter if we haven't spoken in weeks, months, or years. You've always had my back and have always seen the good in me. Thank you for that pep talk you gave me at your graduation. Seeing you with tears in your eyes and telling me how great of a man I was, really resonated with me. It hit me in my soul. I knew that God placed you in my life for a reason. I still remember that Bible verse you told me, Matthew 25-27: "Therefore I tell you, do not worry about your life, what you will eat or drink; or about your body, what you will wear. Is not life more than food, and the body more than clothes? Look at the birds of the air; they do not sow or reap or store away in barns, and yet your God feeds them. Are you not much more valuable than they?" It was just what I needed to hear, and it got me to stop worrying about the things I could not control. Thank you for always being there and not passing judgement on me. Thank you for making me chase my dreams rather than settling for the safe route. I love you, bro. I can't wait to join together to implement our next step. We're going to do great things because God has favored us. I love you, bro. Thank you.

To my best friend Erik Coleman, we have been through everything together. We've been hungry together, we've fought together, we've been questioned by the police together, allegedly. We've done it all. I love you, bro. You are really my brother from another mother. It's a good thing God didn't make you 6'2", or else you probably wouldn't have had the heart that you did. If I had to choose one person on earth to be in a foxhole with, it's you. Number one, we're going to get out; and number two, I'd hate to be on the opposing side of you. You may be the toughest SOB I know, but you're also the gentlest soul I know. You put the welfare of others well before your own. I have watched you lay your life on the line to save another's. You're an amazing leader, brother, father, husband, friend, and brother. You have helped me through the stickiest of situations, and I thank God for sending me a bodyguard in you. I love you, bro. Congratulations on opening up your new Clinic. God willing, we will have to get the families together more. Thank you for being patient with me and for being a true friend. I love you.

To my Dynasty Brothers Jason David and Karl Paymah, I'm thankful for our relationship and your patience with me. You all played while I wasn't good enough and needed to redshirt. I messed up the plan, but you still stuck with me. Thank you for not giving up on me.

To Jason, I truly appreciate your guidance and wisdom. You experienced the Transition before we did and now I know it must have been extremely difficult on you. I'm sorry I wasn't there for you as you have been there for me. You are the model for success and I pray that God continues to bless you, your family, and S.T.A.R.S. You are my role model and I want to be like you when I grow up. Thank you, and I love you.

To Karl, where do I start? You know me better than anyone. You have seen my highest highs and my lowest lows. I'm sure you are probably holding a manila envelope addressed to the White House just in case I say something you don't agree with. I love you, bro. We have been through everything—and I mean everything. You'll probably write a book, television show, and movie script based on our experiences. I'm sure they'll make you millions of dollars; and for the record, it's all true. Thank you for being my wingman, and thank you for the give and go's we executed perfectly. I love you, bro.

To my brother Devard Darling, your circumstance and situation brought you to us, but I'm thankful God blessed us with your presence. Your story, your testimony, and your life is an example of faith. God has blessed you and your family, and I'm thankful that you have allowed us into your heart. To call me your brother means more to me than you could ever know. I love you, bro. I look forward to us joining in on some businesses in the near future and also getting the families together. It's past due, and I really need it. Thank you for being my brother.

To Coach Fred Shavies, I appreciate you for being a stand up individual. The discussions we have are always on another level. Your openness is an admirable trait. God willing, we'll be able travel together now that my book is done, and go see some of those Masjids around the world that you have photographed. I appreciate and love you, bro.

To Lamont Thompson and Marcus Trufant, thank you for showing some young punks what it meant to grind for their dreams. You were the standard. I remember first walking onto the campus in Pullman and seeing you do football drills. I had never seen two individuals look so graceful while working out. It's not a surprise that you both were high NFL draft picks and enjoyed great careers in the pros. Thank you for setting the standard. I love you guys.

To Matt Ware, Michael Adams, Rashad Johnson, and Trumaine McBride, thank you for riding with me. We had some great times in Arizona. When I daydream and reminisce, I always go back to our time in AZ; sitting on a knee, watching practice, but talking about something that had nothing to do with football. Thank you for keeping me grounded. Thank you for holding me to a higher standard. You guys didn't let me be like everyone else and fit in. You made me standout. Thank you for those heartfelt conversations and messages. You guys kept me sane. Although we all wanted to start, we held each other accountable and kept it funky. I still think we were the best second unit in NFL history. At least that's what I tell myself. Thank you for welcoming me into the group, and thank you for being my brothers. I love you all. God willing, we can get the families together soon. We all need to move to Mike's neighborhood and raise our families together. I'm sure that would be worthy of another book. Thank you.

To Brother Leo Beard, thank you for keeping me out of trouble. You would drop me off at home and shield me away from what the crowd was doing. You knew I had a special future and you didn't want me to throw it away by making a stupid decision. I appreciate you for that. You have a great family, and we'll have to go play golf now that I'm finished with my book.

To Coach Troy Adams, thank you for your honesty and belief in me. You are a man's man. Every time you talked to Aqil, I could tell you were also talking to me. I needed every bit of your advice. You came into our lives at a perfect time. God's timing is always perfect, and I'm thankful that He placed you in our lives. Now that I'm done with this book, it's time to plan that go-kart event at Adams Motorsports Park! I love you, Coach. Thank you.

To Sister Souljah, thank you for being real. Thank you for your soulful conversations and encouragements. Thank you for believing in me. Thank you for your words and compliments. Your words, as a world renowned author, means more than the average person. You telling me that I had what it takes to write a book really inspired me. Thank you for that. I look forward to working with you soon so that you can tell the story that needs to be told. I truly appreciate your messages and your phone calls. You have served as my psychiatrist and counselor on many occasions. Thank you for allowing me to let my hair down with you. It's always therapeutic when I speak with you. Your demeanor and words are calming to the soul. Thank you for your book *A Deeper Love Inside: The Porsche Santiaga Story*. I wasn't a fan of fiction, until I read it. I'm hooked, and I can't wait to read your Midnight series. I am truly grateful for your positive voice in my family's life. Thank you.

To Terrell Thomas, a million thank yous. You texted me on my birthday in 2015 and asked how the book was coming. You didn't know it, but I hadn't picked it up in months. I had just about given up on it. I was frustrated and ready to quit, but when you asked me with true sincerity, it reignited the fire. I immediately got to work, and a month later I met brother Saad. A few months later, I met Sister Baiyinah. They read my work and helped shape it into what it is today. None of that happens if I don't get that text from you. I am indebted to you, my brother. I pray that God blesses you and your family in ways that only He can. May God shower upon you his unlimited grace, mercy, and blessings. Thank you.

To Saad Yousuf, thank you for your email. You resurrected this book and turned it from a project to a process and now to a published work of art. Thank you for believing in me and my work. Thank you for loving for your brother what you loved for yourself. Thank you for your passion and commitment. Thank you for our coffee shop talks. They were always timely. *In shaa Allah* we can get together soon. Salaams

To Sister Baiyinah (Umm Zakiyyah), thank you. You were truly sent from Allah. I had taken my manuscript as far as I could and you showed up and took it to where it needed to go. Your attention to detail, professionalism, and talent are second to none. You are knowledgeable and willing to share that knowledge with anyone eager to learn. I thank you for being patient with me and my many errors, shortcomings, and mistakes. Thank you for taking a chance on a guy that many others declined to work with. I pray that you are rewarded with what is best for you and your family, in this life and the next. You have a fan, a client, and a brother for life. Thank you.

To Swin Cash and Nate Jackson, your books *Humble Journey: More Precious than Gold* and *Slow Getting Up*, inspired me to write this book. Thank you for telling your stories, because it gave me the confidence to tell mine.

To Greg Langin, the coolest soccer dad I know, thank you for welcoming me into the soccer dad fraternity. Our conversations during soccer practice always gave me a jump. You pushed me to continue writing and to continue working on my craft. I appreciate you taking your time to read this story and give me your feedback. I am forever thankful for you and your family. We'll have to get our families together and celebrate. Thank you again.

To my LA Fitness gym buddies, thank you for your patience, conversation, camaraderie and competitive spirit. You gave me an opportunity to be one of the guys again. I look forward to getting back in the gym with you guys and sharing more of my story. Thank you again.

Thank you to my family for the unwavering support in not just my writing, but my life. I know you have suffered and sacrificed a great deal to allow me to live my dream and compile this extensive work on Transition. I pray Allah blesses you all.

Thank you to my friends, supporters, and acquaintances to whom I expressed my desire to write this book, and you encouraged me to do so.

Thank you to the many individuals who have supported Husain and me throughout our careers.

Thank you to the Washington State University fan base and alumni who have shown their unequivocal love and support for me and Husain.

Thank you to my NFL family for the experience. I hope this meets your level of satisfaction and you feel as though I told the story the right way.

And for all others who have helped me along my way or issued a positive salutation in my direction, thank you. I truly appreciate you for sharing with me something I can never repay. Your time. Peace, and Be Blessed.

To all of my friends, family, neighbors, Muslim community members, teammates, coaches, agents, financial advisor, lawyers, CPA, and landlord. Thank you. Thank you for praying for me and my family. I am so very blessed to have so many people in my corner.

Finally, thank you Mrs. Cynthia Hinton. I see that when God wants to truly bless a man, he surrounds him with great women. Mrs. Hinton, I love you so much. You could have given up on me, but you didn't. You could have just done your job as a high school English teacher and just let me fall by the wayside, but you didn't. You could have read my scribbles, marked them with a red F, and moved on, but you didn't. You moved my seat from the back of the class to the front. You made me read aloud, lead discussion groups, and made me READ. You gave me Richard Wright's *Black Boy* during the winter break and told me to write a book report. I thought about having someone else read it and do the paper, but I didn't want to let you down. I read it, and it sparked an interest in me that I didn't know I had. I actually enjoyed reading. You worked with me on my reading and writing, but most importantly, you showed me that you cared. You cared about me. The day I signed my National Letter of Intent to go to Washington State University was one of the best days of my life. Not because I was going to college, but because you told me it was my day. You put away the assignments and told everyone we would celebrate ME. I had never been celebrated until then. Thank you for loving me. You showed me love through your actions, and I am forever grateful. I wish every school had a Cynthia Hinton, but I know that's not the case. You're one of a kind, and I'm fortunate you were placed in my life. I love you, Mrs. Hinton. Thank you.

HT: 6'2"   WT: 220   DOB: 08/20/1983

College: Washington State University

Drafted: Round 1 Pick 1 by ABB

Hometown: Pomona, CA

After a brief seven year stint in the National Football League, Hamza dedicated his time to perfecting his craft as a writer. Abdullah Bros Books took notice of Hamza's dedication and chose him with the first overall pick.

Although many literary agents and publishers said he was raw and not worth the trouble, ABB dismissed those claims and made him the face of their franchise. Hamza has spent the last four years sharpening his tools and preparing for the big stage. With the release of *Hamza Abdullah: Come Follow Me* and *NFL Players: Following Hamza Abdullah*, look for Hamza to have a breakout season in 2017.

Year	Team	Reading	Writing	Research	Interviewing
2013	Abdullah Bros Books	84 Hours	41 Hours	63 Hours	14 Hours
2014	Abdullah Bros Books	517 Hours	647 Hours	310 Hours	27 Hours
2015	Abdullah Bros Books	718 Hours	348 Hours	307 Hours	7 Hours
2016	Abdullah Bros Books	745 Hours	438 Hours	448 Hours	46 Hours

Year	Team	Reading	Writing	Research	Interviewing
	Career Hours Average Per Week	9.7 HPW	6.95 HPW	5.3 HPW	0.4 HPW

COACHING STATISTICS

	Played in the NFL	**Played NCAA Div 1-FBS**
NFL Head Coaches	10 out of 32 (31.25%)	20 out of 32 (62.5%)
NFL O/D Coordinators	16 out of 64 (25%)	44 out of 64 (68.75%)
NFL Assistant Coaches	198 out of 662 (29.9%)	415 out of 662 (62.7%)
NFL General Managers	8 out of 32 (25%)	14 out of 32 (43.75%)

The coaching statistics have been compiled by Mustafa Johnwell and are available in greater detail on www.AbdullahBros.com. Statistics are accurate as of September 11, 2016. Allow a +/- 2% for general oversight.

Abdullah Bros Books
Publisher

Abdullah Bros Books (ABB) aims to educate and enlighten via quality literature created by dedicated individuals.

ABB was born from the desire and passion of the Abdullah Brothers to leave a lasting legacy that will continue to promote and advocate the guiding principle: want for your brother what you want for yourself. By creating literature based in selflessness and leadership, we will be at the forefront in peace relations across the globe. Through the power of the pen, we intend to bridge the gap between individuals and groups with perceived differences. By giving those who are often misrepresented or underrepresented a voice and a seat at the table, we endeavor to tell the whole story. We will focus on stories that represent truth, fairness, and equality.

We want to make sure our readers feel as though you have won every time you pick up one of our books. Through carefully selected content and gifted writers, we aim to be the standard in book publishing. The Abdullah Brothers were raised on the creed, "want for your brother, what you want for yourself." This simple saying has led the brothers to consciously evaluate the totality of their decisions and how they will affect others. Win/win is the only solution to a conflict, relationship, and transaction. We will all win in the end once we see others as brothers and sisters.

We try to put our best foot forward, but we know we may not always execute our objectives as planned. We apologize for our shortcomings and mistakes, and we ask that you forgive us. Our intentions are to provide you with a product, story, and experience that we want for ourselves. Through these intentions, we pray that we begin discussions that lead to meaningful actions. We hope that you won't just sit on the sideline, but that you'll grab your equipment and get into the game.

This is more than a book, it is a movement. Join the movement to better the world, one book at a time.

A Come Follow Me Book

This book is part of our Come Follow Me series. In this series, we feature well-respected individuals in their careers to tell their stories and share the lessons and strategies they have learned in order to sincerely help others. To find out more about the series and upcoming titles in the series, visit www.AbdullahBros.com.

Follow Hamza Abdullah and Abdullah Bros
on Social Media

Platform	Username
twitter	@HamzaAbdullah21
LIKE US ON facebook	Abdullah Brothers
Instagram	@HamzaAbdullah21
YouTube	AbdullahBros
Linked in	Hamza Abdullah

BIBLIOGRAPHY

Abdel Haleem, M. A. S. <u>The Qur'an: A New Translation by M. A. S. Abdel Haleem</u>. New York: Oxford University Press, 2004, 2005, 2010.

Ali, Muhammad and Ali, Hana Yasmeen. <u>The Soul of a Butterfly</u>. New York: Simon & Schuster, 2004.

Bridges, William. <u>The Way of Transition</u>. Cambridge: Da Capo Press, 2001.

Chandler, Steve. <u>17 Lies That are Holding You Back & The Truth That Will Set You Free</u>. Los Angeles: Renaissance Books, 2000.

Chopra, Deepak. <u>The Ultimate Happiness Prescription: 7 Keys to Joy and Enlightenment</u>. New York: Harmony Books, 2009.

Covey, Stephen R. <u>The 7 Habits of Highly Effective People</u>. New York: Simon & Schuster, 1989, 2004.

Enright, Robert D. <u>Forgiveness is a Choice</u>. Washington DC: APA Life Tools, 2001

Sanders, Steve. <u>Training Camp For Life</u>. Cleveland, OH: TCFL Publishing, 2014

Sando, Mike. "Rooney Rule in Reverse: Minority Coaching Hires Have Stalled." *ESPN*. 19 July 2016. 19 July 2016. <<u>http://espn.go.com/nfl/story/_/id/17101097/staggering-numbers-show-nfl-minority-coaching-failure-rooney-rule-tony-dungy</u>>.

Seifert, Kevin. "Ranking the Playing Careers of all 32 NFL Head Coaches." *ESPN*. 23 June 2016. 24 June 2016. <<u>http://espn.go.com/nfl/story/_/id/16378780/ranking-nfl-head-coaches-players-32-1</u>>

Wicks, Robert J. Perspective: The Calm Within The Storm. New York: Oxford University Press, 2014.

"The NFL might have a growing poverty problem." *Burkmont*. 27 October 2015. 16 May 2016. <http://www.burkmont.com/2015/10/the-nfl-might-have-growing-poverty.html>.

"Picking Future Coaches on all 32 NFL Rosters." *ESPN*. 21 June 2016. 24 June 2016. <http://espn.go.com/nfl/story/_/page/32for32x160621/picking-future-coaches-all-32-nfl-rosters-cincinnati-bengals-vontaze-burfict-dallas-cowboys-jason-witten>.

"Probability of Competing Beyond High School." *NCAA*. 25 April 2016. 16 May 2016. <http://www.ncaa.org/about/resources/research/football>.

A Memoir. The NFL. A Transition. A Challenge. A Change.

For more resources, visit:
AbdullahBros.com